# LOST SOULS

## 50 NATIONAL PARK DISAPPEARANCES

## EVAN GRANT

FREE REIGN
Publishing

ISBN 13: 979-8-89234-082-3

Free Reign Publishing, LLC
San Diego, CA

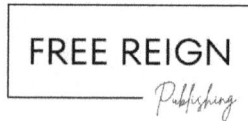

FREE REIGN
*Publishing*

# CONTENTS

# INTRODUCTION

The allure of America's national parks is undeniable. Spanning over 84 million acres, these protected lands offer breathtaking landscapes, diverse ecosystems, and a promise of adventure. However, beneath the surface of this natural beauty lies a more troubling reality: a history of mysterious disappearances that have left families searching for answers and authorities perplexed.

According to data from the National Park Service (NPS), there have been thousands of search and rescue (SAR) missions over the years. In 2017 alone, the NPS reported 3,453 SAR operations, resulting in 1,000 successful rescues and 182 fatalities. Despite these efforts, many cases remain unresolved, with individuals vanishing without a trace.

While the NPS does not maintain a comprehensive public database of all missing persons within its parks, it is estimated that hundreds of people have disappeared under mysterious circumstances. Some reports suggest that over 1,600 individuals have gone missing on federal lands, including national parks, over the past few decades. The reasons behind these disappearances are varied and often baffling, ranging from accidents and natural hazards to more enigmatic causes that defy explanation.

One of the most well-known cases involves the Grand Canyon National Park, which has recorded at least 56 missing persons and six fatalities since 2018. Yosemite National Park, another hotspot for disappearances, lists numerous cold cases, such as the 1981 disappearance of 14-year-old Stacey Anne Arras, who vanished while hiking to take photographs.

These stories of lost souls are more than mere statistics; they are the narratives of real people who set out to explore the wilderness and never returned. *Lost Souls: 50 National Park Disappearances* delves into these haunting tales, offering a closer look at the mysteries that continue to puzzle investigators and captivate the public. Through meticulous research and firsthand accounts, this book aims to shed light on the enigma of these disappearances and honor the memories of those who remain missing in America's beloved national parks.

- Evan Grant
2024

# CHAPTER
# ONE

SAMANTHA "SAM" SAYERS

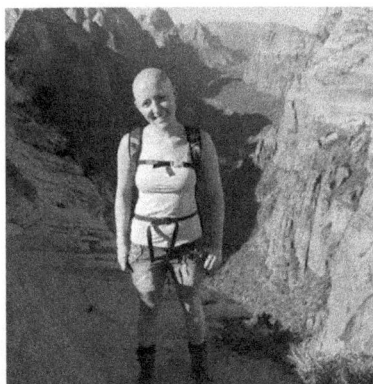

ON AUGUST 1, 2018, SAMANTHA "SAM" Sayers, an experienced 28-year-old hiker, set off on a solo day hike to Vesper Peak in the North Cascades of Washington State. Despite her familiarity with the trail, she never returned. What followed was one of the most extensive and exhaustive search and rescue operations in the state's history, yet no trace of her has been found.

---

Sam Sayers was an avid hiker who had previously tackled challenging routes. On the morning of her disappearance, she left her home in Seattle's Belltown neighborhood, packing light for what she intended to be a routine hike. She had planned to check in with her boyfriend, Kevin Dares, by 6 PM that evening, but she never did.

Vesper Peak is known for its demanding terrain, involving steep switchbacks, boulder fields, and snowfields even in summer. Sam had successfully completed this hike multiple times before, which added to the puzzling nature of her disappearance.

Sam was last seen around 2 PM near the summit by other hikers. She signed the trail register at Sunrise Mine Trail #707, but no one saw her descend. When she failed to check in, Kevin Dares drove to the trailhead and found her car still parked there. He attempted to search for her in the dark but had to retreat after his flashlight broke.

The search for Sam Sayers began immediately and involved numerous agencies and volunteers. Helicopters, drones, search dogs, and ground teams combed the area for weeks. The terrain posed significant challenges, with dangerous crevasses and steep drops making the search perilous. Despite the extensive efforts, no physical evidence, such as her gear or clothing, was found.

Searchers focused on various areas, including Wirtz Basin and Headlee Pass. They inspected snow bridges and crevasses, hoping to find any sign of Sam. Experienced searchers, like Elaina Jorgensen, were baffled by the lack of evidence. Even cadaver dogs brought in to detect human scent found nothing.

Authorities noted that Sam was well-prepared for a day hike but lacked overnight gear. National Park rangers and police considered multiple scenarios, including an accidental fall, exposure to elements, or potential foul play. However, there were no signs of struggle or evidence pointing to any specific theory.

Snohomish County Sheriff's Office led the search operations, and the intensity of their efforts was unprecedented. At one point, over 70 searchers were deployed daily. Despite this, the rugged terrain and variable weather conditions hampered their efforts.

Several hikers reported seeing Sam on the day she disappeared. Climbers at the summit around 2 PM recalled seeing her but noticed nothing unusual. These accounts were consistent with her intended timeline, but no one saw her during the descent, which remains one of the most perplexing aspects of her case.

The mystery of Sam Sayers' disappearance has led to numerous theories:

1. Accidental Fall: One prevalent theory is that Sam might have slipped and fallen into a crevasse or off a cliff. The area is known for its treacherous terrain, and an accident could explain the lack of visible evidence. However, searchers argue that they would have found some trace, such as clothing or gear, in the vicinity of a fall.

2. Wildlife Encounter: Another theory involves a possible encounter with wildlife. While less likely, given the lack of evidence of such an event, it's considered a possibility in the wilderness.

3. Intentional Disappearance: Some speculate that Sam might have chosen to disappear voluntarily. This theory is less supported by those who knew her well, as she had no history of such behavior and was looking forward to future plans.

4. Foul Play: Although there is no direct evidence pointing to foul play, it hasn't been entirely ruled out. The remoteness of the area and the lack of witnesses make this theory difficult to confirm or dismiss.

5. Environmental Factors: The weather and terrain conditions on Vesper Peak can change rapidly. An unexpected weather event or environmental hazard could have contributed to her disappearance.

In the months following her disappearance, Kevin Dares and Sam's family continued to search tirelessly. They raised funds, coordinated volunteer searches, and maintained hope. Social media played a significant role, with the hashtag #FindSamSayers becoming a rallying point for supporters.

Despite these efforts, the official search was scaled back after several months. The case remains open, with occasional new searches and tips being investigated. The community of hikers and rescuers involved has expressed frustration and sorrow over the lack of closure.

––––––––

The disappearance of Sam Sayers is a stark reminder of the unpredictable nature of wilderness areas and the limitations of even the most thorough search and rescue operations. Her case remains one of the most enigmatic in the history of the North Cascades, leaving a lasting impact on those who knew her and the broader community of outdoor enthusiasts.

While the official search efforts have ceased, the hope of finding answers persists. Sam's story continues to resonate, inspiring caution and respect for the natural environments we seek to explore. The search for Sam Sayers is a testament to human resilience and the enduring quest for answers in the face of mystery.

# CHAPTER
# TWO

## TERRENCE WOODS

TERRENCE WOODS JR., a 27-year-old from Maryland, was an accomplished production assistant with an impressive resume in television production. Woods had worked on prominent projects like "The

Voice UK" and "Saving Africa's Elephants: Hugh and the Ivory War." Described by those who knew him as reliable, dedicated, and without any known mental health issues, Woods's disappearance during a shoot in Idaho remains one of the most perplexing unsolved cases in recent years.

––––––––

Woods arrived in Idaho after spending time on location in Montana. He was part of a team filming a documentary on abandoned gold mines for Raw TV, a British production company. Woods had communicated regularly with his family, assuring them he had arrived safely and was ready to work.

In the days preceding his disappearance, Woods began to exhibit uncharacteristic behavior. Crew members reported that he seemed anxious and even attempted to grab a drone from the sky, actions that were highly unusual for him. This culminated in what was described as an anxiety attack on the morning of October 5, a claim disputed by his family who insisted he had no history of such issues.

On October 5, 2018, around 5:30 PM, as the crew was finishing their day's work at the Penman Mine near the ghost town of Orogrande, Woods told a local woman assisting with transport that he needed to use the bathroom. Without warning, he dropped his radio and belt and sprinted down a steep cliff into the dense forest. Despite attempts by the crew to follow him, the challenging terrain made it impossible. The crew reported him missing to the Idaho County Sheriff's Office that evening.

The search for Woods was extensive, involving multiple agencies, dog teams, ground searchers, and helicopters. For seven days, search and rescue teams scoured the area but found no trace of Woods. His phone records, bank accounts, and social media accounts showed no activity since his disappearance, leading authorities to classify the case as a missing person.

The initial police reports suggested that Woods had a mental breakdown, as indicated by the 911 call logs. However, his family vehemently denied any history of mental health issues, describing him as a well-adjusted and successful young man. Friends and colleagues also attested to his stable mental state, questioning the narrative of a sudden breakdown.

Friends and family have raised concerns about the work environment at Raw TV, suggesting it may have contributed to Woods's distress. According to his parents, Woods had expressed a desire to leave the shoot early, citing a family emergency that was later confirmed to be false. This has led to speculation that Woods felt unsafe or pressured on set. Reports have surfaced of a toxic culture within the production company, with some former employees describing a harsh and stressful work environment.

While the Idaho County Sheriff's Office found no evidence of foul play, Woods's family remains skeptical. They have questioned the thoroughness of the investigation and the cooperation of Raw TV. Terrence Woods Sr. has repeatedly asked why professional medical assistance was not sought if his son was indeed experiencing severe emotional distress. Additionally, Woods's father expressed frustration over the lack of transparency from Raw TV, including the refusal to provide names of the crew members who were present at the time of his son's disappearance.

Woods's family has continued to seek answers and has hired private investigators to probe deeper into the case. Social media campaigns have been launched to raise awareness and gather information, with friends and supporters sharing updates and urging anyone with information to come forward. The case has garnered significant media attention, with coverage from various news outlets and true crime blogs.

Despite the passage of time, the search for Terrence Woods Jr. remains active. His family persists in their quest for answers, driven by the belief that crucial information has yet to surface. They have reached out to various organizations and utilized social media platforms to keep the public informed and engaged.

Those who knew Woods described him as a quiet,

kind, and caring individual. Rochelle Newman, a friend and colleague, met Woods at a networking event and remembered him as someone who enjoyed meeting new people and had friends worldwide. She, along with other friends, has been vocal about the discrepancies in the narrative provided by Raw TV and the police. Cassandra Hall-Alexander, another colleague, echoed these sentiments, emphasizing that Woods had always exceeded expectations and had never shown signs of mental health issues.

Terrence Woods Sr. has been a relentless advocate for his son, questioning the actions and statements of those involved in the investigation. He has sought surveillance footage to confirm his son's arrival in Idaho and has been critical of the lack of immediate medical intervention if Woods was indeed experiencing a mental breakdown. Woods's family believes there may have been foul play or significant negligence on the part of the production company.

While some crew members reported Woods behaving erratically, his family and close friends strongly dispute this, suggesting that any claims of mental health issues are unfounded. This theory, while initially plausible to some, lacks substantial evidence given Woods's history and the accounts of those who knew him best.

The work environment theory posits that Woods may have been under significant stress due to the toxic culture at Raw TV. This theory gains credibility from multiple reports of the production company's harsh work conditions. Woods's fabricated story about a family emergency could indicate his desperation to leave the stressful environment, pointing towards this theory as a significant factor in his disappearance.

The theory of foul play or gross negligence by the production company has been suggested by Woods's family. They argue that the company's lack of cooperation and transparency, coupled with the disappearance occurring in a remote and difficult-to-access area, raises suspicions. While the sheriff's office found no evidence supporting foul play, the family's concerns highlight potential gaps in the investigation.

———

The disappearance of Terrence Woods Jr. is a case fraught with unanswered questions and complex emotions. Despite exhaustive search efforts and ongoing investigations, his fate remains unknown. The conflicting accounts of his mental state, the work environment, and the circumstances of his disappearance have left a trail of uncertainty and speculation.

Woods's family continues to advocate for a deeper investigation and broader public awareness, hoping that new information will come to light. The case serves as a somber reminder of the challenges and dangers inherent in remote filming locations and the need for thorough investigative practices in such environments.

If you have any information regarding the disappearance of Terrence Woods Jr., please contact the Idaho County Sheriff's Office at (208) 983-1100. The family and investigators remain hopeful that new leads will eventually provide the answers they so desperately seek.

# CHAPTER
# THREE

SHIRLEY BAUMANN

ON JULY 20, 2020, 61-year-old Shirley Baumann embarked on a hiking trip near Lake Blethen in the Mt. Baker-Snoqualmie National Forest. An experienced hiker, Shirley planned a two-day trek but failed to return as scheduled on July 22. Her disappearance has since become a perplexing case, involving extensive search efforts, eyewitness accounts, and various theories about what might have happened to her.

Shirley Baumann was known for her love of the outdoors. She was equipped with her brown sunglasses, reading glasses, and a cellphone that was not a smartphone. Despite her preparedness and experience, something went drastically wrong on that hike, leading to her becoming one of the numerous missing persons in America's national parks.

Shirley's hike began at the Quartz Creek Trailhead, located in a remote part of the Snoqualmie River Middle Fork area near North Bend, Washington. According to initial reports, Baumann did not drive herself to the trailhead; she was dropped off by a friend. This was a common practice for her, given the logistical challenges of solo hiking in remote areas. She planned to camp overnight near the trail, possibly at a makeshift site close to Lake Blethen.

When Shirley did not return on July 22, her friend reported her missing. The King County Sheriff's Office and various Search and Rescue (SAR) teams launched an extensive search operation. The SAR teams, including volunteers and professionals, devoted over 3,000 hours to searching the treacherous terrain. The area around Quartz Creek Trail is known for its rugged and challenging landscape, featuring cliffs, dense forests, and old mining sites.

Despite the extensive efforts, the search yielded limited results. Search dogs were able to pick up her scent near her campsite and along the trail, but there were no definitive signs of Shirley herself. Her camping gear was found intact, indicating she had set up camp as planned. However, her cellphone and other personal items were missing, adding to the mystery.

Several hikers reported seeing a woman matching Shirley's description near the Quartz Creek Trail around the time of her disappearance. One hiker, Andrea, recounted a strange experience in the area just weeks after Shirley went missing. She described finding fresh bear scat and signs of animal activity near the trail, which led her to believe that wildlife might have played a role in Shirley's disappearance. However, there were no signs of a bear attack or any disturbance at Shirley's campsite that would suggest such an encounter.

Another eyewitness, Valerie, mentioned that it was unusual to see someone hiking alone in that remote area, which made Shirley memorable to those who saw her. This raised questions about whether she might have encountered someone else on the trail, potentially leading to foul play.

Several theories have emerged regarding Shirley Baumann's disappearance:

1. Accidental Injury or Fall: Given the challenging terrain, one plausible theory is that Shirley might have slipped or fallen, resulting in an injury that left her incapacitated. The cliffs and rugged landscape of the Quartz Creek Trail make this a likely scenario. However, the lack of any physical evidence or remains casts doubt on this theory.

2. Wildlife Encounter: Another theory suggests that Shirley might have had a dangerous encounter with wildlife. The fresh bear scat found by Andrea supports this possibility. However, typically such encounters would leave more evidence, such as disturbed ground or remains, neither of which were found in Shirley's case.

3. Foul Play: Some speculate that Shirley might have encountered another person with ill intentions. The remote nature of the trail and the fact that she was alone make this a concerning possibility. Despite this, there is no direct evidence pointing to foul play, and the area did not have any reported suspicious activity at the time.

4. Getting Lost or Disoriented: It's possible that Shirley became lost or disoriented while hiking. The dense forest and numerous unmarked paths could easily confuse even an experienced hiker. If she wandered off the trail, she could have succumbed to the elements or been unable to find her way back.

5. Suicide: Although less likely, some have considered the possibility that Shirley might have intended to end her life. There is no evidence to support this theory, and her friends and family have stated that she had no history of mental health issues or suicidal tendencies.

The case remains open, with periodic searches and investigations continuing as new information becomes available. The King County Sheriff's Office has urged anyone with information about Shirley's disappearance to come forward, highlighting the importance of community involvement in solving such cases.

Shirley's disappearance has had a profound impact on her family and the local hiking community. It serves as a stark reminder of the dangers inherent in solo hiking and the unpredictable nature of wilderness areas. The case has also sparked discussions about the need for better safety measures and communication tools for hikers, especially in remote regions.

The disappearance of Shirley Baumann is a haunting mystery that underscores the potential dangers of exploring the great outdoors. Despite the extensive search efforts and various theories, Shirley's fate remains unknown. Her case joins a long list of unexplained disappearances in America's national parks, each one a poignant reminder of the fine line between adventure and peril.

The search for Shirley continues, driven by the hope that one day, the truth about what happened to her will be uncovered. Until then, her story remains a testament to the enduring mystery of the wild and the resilience of those who seek to unravel it.

# CHAPTER
# FOUR

BRYCE HERDA

BRYCE FLORIAN HERDA'S disappearance remains one of the most perplexing and haunting cases in the history of missing persons in national parks. On April 9, 1995, six-year-old Bryce vanished while hiking with his family on Shi Shi Beach, located within the Makah Indian Reservation near Neah Bay, Washington. Despite extensive search efforts and numerous theories, Bryce's fate remains a mystery.

————

Bryce Herda was a Native American boy with a medium build, standing at four feet tall and weighing around sixty pounds at the time of his disappearance. He had distinctive physical features, including a scar on his forehead, a freckle on his right temple, and a light-colored birthmark on his upper thigh. On the day he disappeared, Bryce was wearing a white T-shirt, green pants, white socks, and red and black Mighty Morphin Power Rangers shoes.

The Herda family was enjoying a day out on Shi Shi Beach, a remote and rugged stretch of coastline known for its scenic beauty and challenging terrain. As the family began to make their way back up a trail to exit the beach, Bryce lagged behind, unable to keep up with the steeper sections of the trail. His family decided to let him remain on the beach, planning to meet him at a designated spot once they had completed the ascent. When they returned to the beach, Bryce was nowhere to be found.

An extensive search was immediately launched involving multiple agencies, including the Neah Bay

Police Department, the Coast Guard, and local volunteers. Tracker dogs were brought in to follow Bryce's scent, and divers searched the waters off the beach. Footprints believed to be Bryce's were found, but they seemed to start and stop intermittently, leading searchers to consider a variety of possible scenarios.

Despite these efforts, no trace of Bryce was ever found. The rugged and remote nature of the area, combined with the high tides and powerful waves, complicated the search efforts significantly. Theories about his disappearance ranged from accidental drowning to abduction, but no conclusive evidence supported any specific outcome.

---

Theories and Speculations

- Accidental Drowning: One of the most widely considered theories is that Bryce was swept out to sea by a rogue wave. The Pacific Ocean along the Olympic Coast is known for its unpredictable and dangerous surf conditions. However, despite extensive underwater searches, no remains were found, which casts some doubt on this theory.
- Abduction: Bryce's parents strongly believed that their son was abducted. Given the

proximity of the Makah Indian Reservation, some speculated that Bryce might have been taken by someone familiar with the area. This theory was supported by the lack of physical evidence pointing to an accident. However, there were no witnesses or credible leads to substantiate claims of abduction.

- Wandering Off: Another possibility is that Bryce, left alone on the beach, might have wandered off into the dense forest surrounding the area. The wilderness around Shi Shi Beach is vast and difficult to navigate, especially for a young child. Although this scenario is plausible, the intensive search efforts would likely have found some trace of him if he had wandered into the forest.

- Foul Play: Given the area's remoteness and the presence of transient communities along some of the nearby trails, there were concerns about potential foul play. The Ozette Trail, which connects to the Shi Shi Beach area, is known to have several homeless camps. This led some to speculate that Bryce could have encountered someone with ill intentions. However, investigations into these communities did not yield any significant leads.

Bryce's disappearance had a profound impact on the

local community and the nation. The case highlighted the need for better safety measures and awareness when visiting remote and rugged natural areas. Bryce's family, particularly his grandfather who was the chief of police in the area at the time, has continued to advocate for awareness and search efforts.

The case remains open, with occasional renewed interest when new information or technological advancements in search and rescue operations occur. The National Center for Missing and Exploited Children continues to list Bryce Herda as missing, and age-progressed images are periodically released to help in identifying him if he is still alive.

# CHAPTER
# FIVE

## JAMES PRUITT

JAMES PRUITT, a 70-year-old hiker from Etowah, Tennessee, disappeared while hiking in Rocky Mountain National Park on February 28, 2019. His disappearance triggered an extensive search operation involving numerous search and rescue teams, yet no trace of him has been found.

———

James Pruitt was an experienced hiker who had visited Rocky Mountain National Park several times before. His familiarity with the area made his disappearance even more perplexing. On February 22, 2019, Pruitt arrived at the park for his third winter visit in three years. Over the next few days, he engaged in multiple hikes, often in the Bear Lake area. His last known contact was on the morning of February 28, when he set out for a day hike from the Glacier Gorge Trailhead.

Pruitt's vehicle was found on March 3, 2019, parked at the Glacier Gorge Trailhead at an elevation of 9,240 feet. His family confirmed he had planned to hike on February 28 but did not intend to stay overnight. The discovery of his unattended vehicle, coupled with no subsequent contact, prompted immediate concern and the initiation of search operations.

The initial search began on March 3, involving U.S. Park Rangers who quickly expanded their efforts to include various search and rescue teams. These teams, including Larimer County Search and Rescue, Rocky Mountain Rescue Group, and the Colorado Search and Rescue Board, conducted extensive searches across approximately 15 square miles. The search areas encompassed the Glacier Gorge drainage, Loch Vale drainage, and Glacier Creek drainage. Specific focus was given to heavily forested areas near Bear Lake and the Glacier Gorge Trailhead, as well as regions around Nymph Lake, Dream Lake, Lake Haiyaha, and the Loch/Mills Junction.

Search conditions were challenging due to the harsh winter weather. Over two feet of snow had fallen between February 28 and March 3, making the terrain difficult to navigate and any potential tracks nearly impossible to detect. Search teams had to contend with chest-deep snow in some areas, and strong wind gusts up to 40 miles per hour further complicated the efforts.

Despite the extensive search efforts, which included aerial reconnaissance by a multi-mission aircraft from the State of Colorado, no clues were found. The search involved around 50 personnel at its peak, with special-ized dog teams and various search and rescue organiza-tions contributing to the efforts.

Rangers and searchers noted the particularly chal-lenging conditions of the search area. The heavy snowfall not only hindered the search but also likely covered any evidence that might have indicated Pruitt's whereabouts. According to park officials, the likelihood of finding clues was significantly diminished due to the extreme weather conditions during the critical days following his disappearance.

There were no direct eyewitness accounts of Pruitt on

the day of his disappearance. The last confirmed sighting was by his family before he left for his hike on February 28. Park rangers appealed to the public for any information from hikers who might have been in the Glacier Gorge and Bear Lake areas around the time Pruitt went missing. Despite this, no substantial leads were obtained.

Several theories have been proposed regarding James Pruitt's disappearance:

1. Accidental Injury or Fall: Given the rugged terrain and harsh weather conditions, one of the most plausible theories is that Pruitt may have slipped or fallen, sustaining injuries that prevented him from seeking help. The heavy snowfall could have quickly concealed any signs of such an accident.

2. Hypothermia: The combination of Pruitt's age, the cold weather, and the snow-covered landscape raises the possibility of hypothermia. If Pruitt became disoriented or lost, he could have succumbed to the cold before rescuers could reach him.

3. Animal Encounter: Although less likely, an encounter with wildlife cannot be entirely ruled out. Rocky Mountain National Park is home to various wildlife, including mountain lions and bears, which could pose a threat to a lone hiker.

4. Intentional Disappearance: While there is no evidence to suggest that Pruitt intended to disappear,

this theory remains a part of the broader speculation due to the lack of concrete evidence regarding his fate. However, this theory is considered unlikely by both family and investigators.

Search efforts for James Pruitt continued intermittently throughout the summer and fall of 2019. Smaller search teams revisited specific segments of the search area, which by then had experienced significant visitor activity. Unfortunately, these additional efforts yielded no new clues.

In October 2019, another coordinated search was conducted, focusing on off-trail areas in the Prospect Canyon drainage and the Glacier Gorge drainage above Jewel Lake. Despite these renewed efforts, no evidence was found to provide any answers about Pruitt's disappearance.

———

The disappearance of James Pruitt remains an unsolved mystery. Despite extensive search and rescue efforts and numerous theories about what might have happened, no definitive evidence has been found to explain his fate. Pruitt's case underscores the unpredictable and often perilous nature of wilderness areas, even for experienced hikers. The Rocky Mountain National Park Service continues to investigate and remains hopeful that future efforts or new information may eventually provide answers to this enduring mystery.

# CHAPTER
## SIX
JACOB GRAY

ON APRIL 6, 2017, Jacob Randall Gray, a 22-year-old from Santa Cruz, California, vanished in Olympic National Park, Washington. Jacob was an adventurous young man, well-acquainted with the outdoors, who had set out on a cross-country biking expedition aimed at reaching Vermont, where his brother lived. His journey, however, came to an abrupt and mysterious end when his bicycle and camping gear were found abandoned along the Sol Duc River.

----

Jacob Gray began his trip on April 5, 2017, leaving from Port Townsend, Washington, with a bike and a trailer loaded with camping equipment. His plan was ambitious: to bike across the country, a testament to his adventurous spirit and love for the wilderness. The following day, his bike and gear were discovered approximately 6.5 miles up the Sol Duc Hot Springs Road, raising immediate concerns about his whereabouts.

Rangers from Olympic National Park conducted an initial search on April 6 and 7, focusing on the area around the Sol Duc River where Jacob's belongings were found. Despite these efforts, there was no sign of Jacob, leading to an expansion of the search operation.

The search for Jacob Gray was extensive, involving numerous agencies and volunteers. Olympic National Park Law Enforcement Rangers, Clallam County Sheriff's Search and Rescue, Olympic Mountain Rescue, and various volunteer groups all participated. Search dogs were also employed to comb the area for any trace of Jacob. Despite these efforts, the search yielded no results in the immediate aftermath.

Randy Gray, Jacob's father, quickly became a central

figure in the search. Leaving his home in Santa Cruz, Randy immersed himself in the efforts to find his son, often braving dangerous conditions along the Sol Duc River. His commitment was unwavering; he combed the area tirelessly, aided by friends, family, and volunteers from the community.

The search was not without its challenges. The rugged terrain of Olympic National Park, combined with the dense forests and treacherous river conditions, made the operation particularly difficult. Swiftwater rescue experts suggested that if Jacob had fallen into the river, his chances of survival would have been slim, especially given the cold water and strong currents.

On August 10, 2018, over a year after Jacob's disappearance, a significant breakthrough occurred. A field crew consisting of Olympic National Park employees and volunteers discovered clothing and equipment in a remote part of the park near Hoh Lake. Law enforcement rangers conducted a thorough search the following day and found skeletal remains, which were later confirmed through dental records to be Jacob's.

The location of Jacob's remains was approximately 10 miles from where his bike and gear were initially found. This discovery provided some closure to his family but also raised further questions about how Jacob ended up so far from his last known location and what might have happened in the intervening time.

Several theories have emerged regarding Jacob's

disappearance and death. One of the primary theories suggests that Jacob may have succumbed to the elements. The harsh conditions of Olympic National Park, including its cold and unpredictable weather, could have played a significant role in his fate. The area where Jacob's remains were found is known for its challenging terrain, which could have contributed to his disorientation and eventual demise.

Another theory revolves around the possibility of an accident. Given that Jacob was found with his gear intact and no immediate signs of foul play, it's plausible that he may have suffered a fall or injury that prevented him from seeking help. The rugged landscape of the park, with its steep cliffs and dense forests, presents numerous hazards for even the most experienced outdoorsmen.

The Gray family, particularly Jacob's father, Randy, played a crucial role in the search efforts. Randy's dedication was nothing short of extraordinary; he sold his home in Santa Cruz, bought a camper, and essentially lived in the Olympic Peninsula to continue searching for his son. His relentless pursuit included diving into the Sol Duc River, searching caves, and exploring remote areas far beyond the initial search zones.

Randy's determination was also supported by the local community and volunteers, who joined the search and offered their resources. This collective effort underscores the profound impact Jacob's disappearance had on those who knew him and the broader community.

The disappearance and subsequent discovery of Jacob Gray's remains in Olympic National Park is a tragic story of loss, mystery, and the relentless pursuit of answers by a devoted father. While the discovery of Jacob's remains provided some closure, the exact circumstances of his death remain unclear, leaving a lasting impact on his family and all who were involved in the search efforts.

# CHAPTER
# SEVEN

FERN LOVETT BAIRD

FERN LOVETT BAIRD, a 63-year-old experienced hiker from Park City, Utah, disappeared on October 19, 2020, while hiking near the Prairie Creek Trailhead in the Sawtooth National Forest, Idaho. Baird, a real estate broker, was known for her love of hiking and typically adhered strictly to trails, avoiding risky shortcuts or off-trail exploration.

On the day she vanished, Baird signed the trail log at 1:17 PM, noting her intention to hike "to the lake and back." The trail, a ten-mile loop, is known for its scenic beauty, featuring small waterfalls and dense forest. She was last seen wearing a light gray jacket, dark pants, gray gloves, a dark mask, and carrying a dark fanny pack. Her vehicle, a 2018 Subaru Crosstrek with the vanity plate "YOPABAG," was found parked at the trailhead.

Baird's disappearance was reported on October 22, 2020, after she failed to check out from her hotel. The Blaine County Sheriff's Office (BCSO) initiated a search operation, involving 40 personnel, including K9 units, drones, Idaho National Guard helicopters, and officers on foot and horseback. The search, which lasted nine days, was hampered by inclement weather, including snow and temperatures dropping to the low teens. Despite these efforts, no trace of Baird was found, and the search was officially suspended on October 30, 2020.

Sheriff Steve Harkins expressed his disappointment, stating, "This is not the outcome we were hoping for, but after ten days of searching, we have exhausted our resources." Since her disappearance, there has been no activity on her bank account, credit cards, or cellular phone.

In June 2021, search efforts were renewed as part of a

training operation by the Blaine County Sheriff's SAR. The team searched the Prairie Lakes Trail, a location two miles up the trail noted for its waterfalls. During this operation, a cell phone was found, but it belonged to a local hunter who had lost it the previous fall.

———

Several theories have been proposed regarding Baird's disappearance:

1. Accidental Injury or Death: The most plausible theory is that Baird suffered an accident or became disoriented, leaving the trail and succumbing to the elements. The dense forest and rugged terrain would make locating her difficult.

2. Medical Emergency: It is possible Baird experienced a sudden medical emergency, such as a heart attack or stroke, which incapacitated her before she could seek help.

3. Animal Attack: Although rare, the possibility of an animal attack, such as from a bear or mountain lion, cannot be completely ruled out given the area's wildlife.

4. Foul Play: While there is no evidence to support foul play, it remains a consideration due to the lack of concrete leads or evidence.

5. Voluntary Disappearance: This theory is considered unlikely due to Baird's established social ties,

professional responsibilities, and lack of any apparent motive to vanish voluntarily.

Baird's family, particularly her son Breck, has been actively involved in seeking new information and keeping her case in the public eye. They have urged anyone with information to come forward. The family also offered a reward for information leading to her discovery, hoping to incentivize anyone with potential leads to speak up.

Baird's case has been highlighted by various missing persons organizations, including the Fowler-O'Sullivan Foundation and Texas EquuSearch, to generate more attention and possibly new leads. Despite the extensive search efforts and numerous theories, her disappearance remains unsolved, a mystery that continues to weigh heavily on her family and the community.

———

Despite the extensive efforts of law enforcement and volunteers, the rugged and expansive terrain of the Sawtooth National Forest has kept the mystery of her disappearance unresolved. Authorities continue to encourage anyone with information to contact the Blaine County Sheriff's Office, maintaining hope that new evidence will eventually come to light.

# CHAPTER
# EIGHT

PETER JACKSON

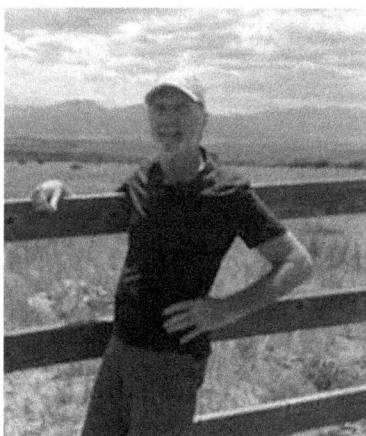

PETER JACKSON, a 74-year-old experienced hiker, disappeared on September 17, 2016, while camping at Yosemite National Park. Jackson was known for his physical fitness and routinely went on moderate to strenuous hikes. He had reserved a spot at White Wolf Campground, where his vehicle was later found. The search for him was extensive but ultimately yielded few clues.

Peter Jackson was last seen at White Wolf Campground, where he had a reservation from September 17 to September 21. He sent a text message to his son on September 17, indicating he was en route to Yosemite. Jackson's son reported him missing on September 26, after not hearing from him for several days.

The National Park Service initiated a search that involved ground teams, search dogs, helicopters, and drones. Despite the intensive efforts, no trace of Jackson was found. The search was suspended on October 2, 2016, due to deteriorating weather conditions and a lack of new leads.

———

Eyewitness Accounts and Theories:

- Eyewitness Accounts: Campers at White Wolf reported not seeing Jackson or any activity at his campsite for several days before he was reported missing. His campsite appeared to be undisturbed, suggesting he left for a hike and did not return.
- Possible Theories: Lost or Injured: Given his age and the challenging terrain of Yosemite,

it's possible Jackson became disoriented or injured during his hike. This theory is supported by his experience in undertaking hikes of similar difficulty, indicating he may have ventured off trail or encountered unexpected difficulties.

- Medical Emergency: Despite being in excellent health, a sudden medical emergency such as a heart attack or stroke could have incapacitated Jackson, making it difficult for him to signal for help or return to his campsite.
- Animal Encounter: Although less likely, given the lack of evidence, an encounter with wildlife could have resulted in his disappearance. However, no signs of a struggle or remains were found during the search.
- Foul Play: While there was no immediate evidence to suggest foul play, this theory cannot be entirely ruled out. The remote nature of Yosemite makes it difficult to entirely discount this possibility.

The search for Peter Jackson involved multiple agencies and extensive resources:

- Ground Teams: Rangers and volunteers

scoured trails, valleys, and potential off-trail routes Jackson might have taken.

- Aerial Surveillance: Helicopters equipped with thermal imaging were used to scan for any signs of life or disturbances in the area.
- Search Dogs: Canine units were deployed to track Jackson's scent, focusing on areas near his last known location and potential hiking routes.

Despite these efforts, no significant clues emerged until 2019, when Jackson's backpack was found between Aspen Valley and Smith Peak. This discovery renewed some interest in the case, but no additional evidence was uncovered to provide clear answers about his fate.

As of now, Peter Jackson's case remains unsolved. The National Park Service continues to treat it as an active missing persons case, following up on any new leads that arise. The case is maintained in a "limited continuous mode," meaning that while active field searches have ceased, any new information will be investigated thoroughly.

Family members and friends have expressed their frustration and sorrow over the lack of closure. They hope that new developments or advanced search technologies might eventually provide answers. Social media and public appeals continue to play a role in keeping the case alive in public memory.

The lack of concrete evidence and the challenging terrain have left his case open and unresolved. Continued awareness and technological advancements may eventually shed light on what happened to Peter Jackson, but until then, his disappearance remains one of Yosemite's enduring mysteries.

# CHAPTER
# NINE

JAMES THOMAS GRIFFIN

JAMES THOMAS GRIFFIN, a 60-year-old resident of Port Angeles, Washington, vanished under perplexing circumstances on December 22, 2014, while hiking in Olympic National Park. Despite extensive search efforts and numerous investigations, the details surrounding his disappearance remain enigmatic.

---

James Griffin was an experienced hiker, familiar with the terrain of Olympic National Park. On December 22, 2014, Griffin set out for a hike to the Olympic Hot Springs, a 2.5-mile trail he frequently traversed. Friends noted that Griffin was in good spirits and looking forward to spending Christmas with his loved ones. However, Griffin did not return as expected, prompting concerns from his family and friends.

Griffin was last seen by other hikers around 4 p.m. at the Olympic Hot Springs. These hikers reported that Griffin appeared to be in good health and spirits. He was seen carrying his backpack, which was known to contain essentials for a day hike, including food, water, snacks, and fire-starters. Despite his familiarity with the trail, Griffin did not make it back to the trailhead where his car, a blue Subaru Forester, was parked.

Griffin's family reported him missing on December 24, 2014, after he failed to show up for Christmas Eve dinner. Olympic National Park authorities immediately launched a search operation. The initial search efforts were extensive, involving park rangers, search and rescue teams, and cadaver dogs. They focused on the area surrounding the Olympic Hot Springs Trail and the vicinity of Griffin's parked car.

Search teams discovered Griffin's backpack on December 25, about 50 feet off the trail and half a mile from the trailhead. Inside the backpack, they found food, water, snacks, and fire-starters, along with an unfinished bag of prepared food nearby. This discovery suggested that Griffin had stopped for a meal, which was unusual given his proximity to the trailhead and the impending darkness.

Despite comprehensive search efforts that included grid searches of a 500-foot radius around the backpack and the use of cadaver dogs, no additional clues were found initially. Heavy rain and cold weather further complicated the search, causing it to be temporarily suspended on December 28.

The search resumed on January 24, 2015, when weather conditions improved. On January 25, Griffin's body was found about a third of a mile from the Olympic Hot Springs Trail, less than a mile from the trailhead. His remains were discovered on a steep, densely forested slope, among downed trees, boulders, and thick brush. Griffin was dressed in long pants, a jacket, and hiking shoes, but notably lacked rain gear, which might have contributed to his vulnerability to the elements.

An autopsy was performed, and while the full results were pending toxicology tests, the preliminary cause of death was attributed to hypothermia. The cold, wet conditions in the park during the time of Griffin's disappearance likely played a significant role. Temperatures had dropped into the low 30s at night, and the area had experienced 0.79 inches of rain in the past week.

———

Eyewitness Accounts and Theories:

1. Medical Emergency or Disorientation: One prevailing theory suggests that Griffin may have suffered a medical emergency that left him disoriented, causing him to wander off the trail. Given that he had a previously injured leg, this theory posits that he might have struggled more than usual, leading to exhaustion and confusion.

2. Hypothermia: Hypothermia can cause severe disorientation, known as "paradoxical undressing," where individuals in the final stages of hypothermia remove their clothing due to a false sensation of warmth. This could explain why Griffin left his pack and wandered away from the trail, ultimately succumbing to the elements.

3. Accidental Fall: The steep, rugged terrain where Griffin's body was found suggests that he might have fallen while trying to navigate the slope. The dense forest and downed trees could have made it difficult for him to find his way back to the trail.

4. Unseen Hazard: Another theory speculates that Griffin might have encountered an unexpected hazard,

such as a wild animal or an unstable part of the trail, which could have caused him to become lost or incapacitated.

5. Foul Play: Although there was no immediate evidence to suggest foul play, the circumstances of Griffin's disappearance have led some to question whether another individual might have been involved. However, no indications of a struggle or presence of others in the area were found.

The investigation into James Griffin's disappearance was thorough, but ultimately, it provided more questions than answers. The autopsy results and toxicology tests confirmed hypothermia as the cause of death, but the exact sequence of events leading to Griffin's fatal hike remains unclear.

James Thomas Griffin's disappearance highlights the unpredictable dangers of hiking in remote and rugged terrains. Despite his experience and preparation, the harsh conditions of Olympic National Park proved fatal. His death serves as a solemn reminder of the importance of preparedness and caution when exploring the wilderness, no matter how familiar the trail might be.

The family and friends of James Thomas Griffin continue to mourn his loss and seek closure. His case remains a poignant example of the mysteries that can occur in the great outdoors, where nature's beauty and danger coexist.

———

The disappearance and subsequent death of James Thomas Griffin is a tragic story and while the exact details of his final moments may never be fully known, the efforts to understand and learn from his experience continue to resonate with hikers, rescuers, and those who hold a deep respect for the wilderness.

Through the lens of Griffin's story, we are reminded of the profound impact of nature's raw power and the enduring quest for answers in the face of inexplicable loss. His legacy prompts us to approach the natural world with both admiration and caution, forever mindful of the thin line between adventure and peril.

THE DISAPPEARANCE of Floyd E. Roberts III is one of the most puzzling cases to emerge from the Grand Canyon National Park. On June 17, 2016, the experienced hiker vanished during a planned nine-day expedition with friends in the park's remote Shivwits Plateau.

———

Floyd E. Roberts III, a 52-year-old experienced hiker from Treasure Island, Florida, set out on a nine-day back-packing trip with his long-time friend, Ned Bryant, and Bryant's daughter, Madeleine. The trio had a well-documented history of hiking together, often tackling challenging terrains with relative ease. They had previously visited the Grand Canyon area in 2011 without incident, making this trip seem like just another adventure for the seasoned hikers.

The group embarked on their journey on June 17, 2016, aiming to explore the rugged and remote Shivwits Plateau in the Grand Canyon-Parashant National Monument. This area is known for its challenging terrain and lack of amenities, making it suitable only for the most prepared and experienced hikers. Their plan was to hike through the region, camp along the way, and exit via Separation Canyon on June 26.

On the afternoon of June 17, the group reached a hill near Kelly Tank. At approximately 4:45 PM, they decided to take different routes around the hill: Bryant and his daughter chose to climb over, while Roberts opted to contour around it. They agreed to meet on the other side. However, Roberts never arrived at the rendezvous point. Concerned, Bryant and his daughter retraced their steps and searched the area but found no sign of Roberts.

Bryant and his daughter camped overnight near the

hill and continued their search the next day. By June 18, they had walked to an area with cellular reception and reported Roberts missing to the National Park Service (NPS). The temperatures during this period were extremely high, ranging from 92 degrees Fahrenheit on the day Roberts went missing to over 110 degrees in the subsequent days. Despite the heat, Roberts had brought two gallons of water and enough food to last a week, which gave hope that he could survive for several days if lost.

The NPS launched an extensive search operation involving multiple agencies, including the Coconino County Search and Rescue, Mohave County search teams, and Grand Canyon-Parashant National Monument personnel. The search area covered over 10 square miles of rugged, brush-covered terrain, making the operation both challenging and dangerous for the search teams. They used helicopters, ground teams, and sniffer dogs to comb the area, but no trace of Roberts was found.

The initial search efforts were intense, but as days passed without any leads, the operation was scaled back on June 24, 2016. The authorities then transitioned to a limited but continuous search mode, keeping an eye out for any new clues that might emerge.

Several potential clues were discovered during the search, but none led to a definitive answer. There were reports of footprints found in the area Roberts was last seen, but searchers could not confirm if they belonged to him. The rugged terrain and thick brush further complicated the search efforts, making it difficult to track any possible trails.

Several theories have emerged over the years regarding Floyd E. Roberts III's disappearance:

1. Accidental Injury or Death: One of the most plausible theories is that Roberts may have suffered an injury or medical emergency that prevented him from reaching the rendezvous point. The extreme heat and rugged terrain could have exacerbated any injuries, making it difficult for him to survive.

2. Misadventure: Given the remote and challenging nature of the area, it's possible that Roberts became disoriented and lost. The Grand Canyon's vastness and the lack of clear landmarks in some areas could easily lead to confusion and misdirection.

3. Foul Play: While there is no evidence to suggest foul play, it cannot be entirely ruled out. The Grand Canyon area has its share of criminal activity, although it is rare in such remote parts.

4. Animal Attack: Though less likely, an animal attack is another consideration. The Grand Canyon is home to various wildlife, including mountain lions and other predators, which could pose a threat to an injured or incapacitated hiker.

5. Voluntary Disappearance: Some speculate that

Roberts might have chosen to disappear voluntarily. However, this theory seems unlikely given his close relationships and the meticulous planning that went into the hike.

The disappearance of Floyd E. Roberts III has had a profound impact on the hiking community and his family. Roberts was known for his experience and preparedness, making his sudden disappearance all the more baffling. The case has raised awareness about the risks associated with hiking in remote areas and the importance of having comprehensive search and rescue plans in place.

Despite the scaled-back official search efforts, the Roberts family and friends have not given up hope. They have continued to push for further searches and investigations, hoping that new technology or information might one day lead to answers. The case remains open, and any new leads or clues are thoroughly investigated by the NPS and other agencies involved.

Despite extensive search efforts and numerous theories, no trace of Roberts has been found, leaving his family and friends without closure. His case continues to captivate and baffle those who hear it.

# CHAPTER
# ELEVEN

## JORGE SERRANO ZALDIVAR

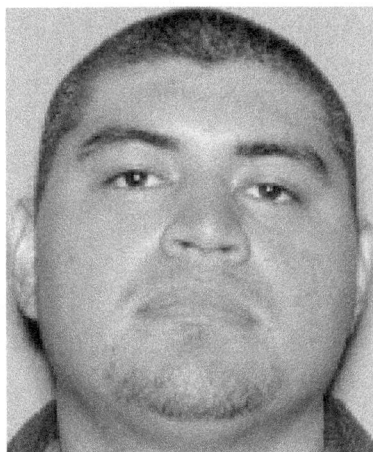

ON JANUARY 25, 2016, Jorge Serrano Zaldivar, a 25-year-old from Rialto, California, disappeared under baffling circumstances. Despite extensive search efforts and ongoing investigations, his whereabouts remain unknown.

———

Jorge Serrano Zaldivar was born on February 6, 1990. He was a Hispanic male, standing 6'1" tall and weighing 270 pounds. He had black hair, brown eyes, and a notable scar on the back of his head. At the time of his disappearance, he was wearing a blue jacket, blue jeans, and gray Nike shoes. Jorge was known to his friends and family as a reliable and loving individual.

On the morning of January 25, 2016, Jorge left his home in Rialto, California, without informing anyone of his plans. He never returned and had no contact with his family or friends since that day. Later that same day, a forest ranger discovered Jorge's blue Honda Civic crashed and abandoned near a shooting range in the Lytle Creek area of the Angeles National Forest, a region known for its rugged terrain and dense forests.

The discovery of his vehicle raised immediate concern. The car had no significant damage that would suggest a major accident, and there were no signs of Jorge at the scene. The area around the car was thoroughly searched by the authorities, but no traces of Jorge were found.

Upon discovering the abandoned vehicle, an extensive search operation was launched by the San Bernardino County Sheriff's Department, with assistance from volunteers and other law enforcement agencies. The search included ground teams, helicopters, and canine units. Despite these efforts, no clues regarding Jorge's whereabouts were uncovered.

The search area was particularly challenging due to the dense forest, steep ravines, and varying elevations. The rugged terrain made it difficult to cover all possible areas where Jorge might have wandered or fallen. Additionally, adverse weather conditions often hampered search efforts, further complicating the operation.

There were few eyewitness accounts related to Jorge's disappearance. The last confirmed sighting of Jorge was when he left his home on the morning of January 25. The forest ranger who found his vehicle reported that it appeared abandoned, with no immediate signs of foul play. This lack of eyewitness accounts or additional evidence at the scene left investigators with minimal leads to follow.

Several theories have emerged over the years regarding what might have happened to Jorge Serrano Zaldivar. These theories range from accidental mishap to foul play and even voluntary disappearance. Here are the primary theories that have been considered:

1. Accidental Misadventure: Given the location where Jorge's car was found, one prevalent theory is that he may have ventured into the forest and succumbed to an accident. The Angeles National Forest is known for its difficult and often dangerous terrain. It's possible that

Jorge could have fallen, gotten injured, or become lost, leading to his inability to return or call for help.

2. Foul Play: Another theory suggests that Jorge might have encountered foul play. This theory posits that someone else could have been involved in his disappearance. However, there has been no concrete evidence to support this theory, and no suspects or persons of interest have been identified by the authorities.

3. Voluntary Disappearance: Some speculate that Jorge might have chosen to disappear voluntarily. This theory is less supported by evidence, as Jorge had no known reasons to leave his life behind and had a close relationship with his family.

4. Mental Health Crisis: There is also the possibility that Jorge experienced a mental health crisis that led him to act erratically. If this were the case, he might have wandered off into the forest without a clear plan, resulting in his disappearance.

The investigation into Jorge Serrano Zaldivar's disappearance has been exhaustive yet fruitless. The Rialto Police Department, which initially handled the case, conducted numerous interviews with Jorge's family, friends, and acquaintances. They reviewed his phone records, social media activity, and any potential financial transactions for clues. Despite these efforts, no new information has come to light.

The case was also covered by various media outlets and featured on websites dedicated to missing persons, such as The Charley Project and Locations Unknown. These platforms helped keep Jorge's case in the public eye, providing a forum for tips and information from the public.

In 2020, an update from the National Missing and Unidentified Persons System (NamUs) reiterated the lack of progress in the case, highlighting the ongoing need for information and public assistance.

Jorge's disappearance has had a profound impact on his family and the local community. His family has been relentless in their search for answers, organizing community searches and working closely with law enforcement. The uncertainty surrounding his fate has been a source of immense pain and frustration for his loved ones.

The community of Rialto, where Jorge lived, has shown solidarity and support for the family. Local media coverage and social media campaigns have kept the case in the public consciousness, with many community members participating in search efforts and vigils.

————

The disappearance of Jorge Serrano Zaldivar remains one of the many unresolved cases that perplex authorities and leave families in a state of perpetual grief and uncertainty. Despite the passage of time, the search for

Jorge continues, driven by the hope that one day, answers will be found, and justice will be served.

As with many missing persons cases, the disappearance of Jorge Serrano Zaldivar underscores the importance of public awareness and community involvement in such investigations. The case remains open, and authorities continue to urge anyone with information to come forward, offering hope that even the smallest detail could lead to a breakthrough.

For now, Jorge Serrano Zaldivar remains among the missing, his story a somber reminder of the mysteries that persist in our world and the enduring strength of those who seek the truth.

# CHAPTER
# TWELVE

## SUSAN ADAMS

THE DISAPPEARANCE of Susan Adams is a perplexing case that has haunted investigators and her loved ones for decades. In September 1990, during a camping and hunting trip in the rugged Selway-Bitterroot Wilderness along the Montana/Idaho border, Susan vanished without a trace.

———

Susan Seymour Adams, a 42-year-old woman from Austin, Texas, embarked on a much-anticipated camping and hunting trip with her husband, Tom, and a group of hunters and guides from Iron Horse Outfitters. The group had spent months planning and researching their excursion, eager to explore the wild beauty of the Selway-Bitterroot Wilderness. They arrived at the campsite on September 22, 1990, and the trip seemed to be going smoothly.

Susan was an experienced outdoorswoman who enjoyed bird watching, a hobby she indulged in during the trip. On the morning of September 30, she told her husband she was going to a nearby meadow to watch birds. She left the campsite around 9:00 AM, carrying only her binoculars and camera, dressed in camouflage-print clothing.

When Susan did not return after a few hours, her husband became concerned and began searching for her. He followed her tracks along the trail leading to the meadow but lost them about 20 yards from the spot. There were no signs of struggle or anything unusual. As hours turned into days, the urgency grew, and an extensive search operation was launched.

The search for Susan Adams was one of the most extensive in Idaho's history. It involved ground teams, aerial searches, and even psychic consultations. Searchers combed through the dense wilderness, walking arm-in-arm across acres of rugged terrain, but no trace of Susan was found. Some believed she might have injured herself, as tracks indicating a possible limp were discovered, but these did not lead to her location.

Despite the intensity of the search, it was eventually called off after several weeks. Sheriff Randy Baldwin, who led the search efforts, expressed his belief that Susan likely succumbed to injuries or other causes related to being lost in the wilderness. He noted that while her remains might still be in the area, future organized searches would probably not be effective in locating them.

Over the years, various theories have emerged regarding Susan's disappearance. Here are some of the most prominent ones:

1. Lost or Injured: The most widely accepted theory is that Susan got lost or injured while bird watching. The area is known for its difficult terrain, and without food, warm clothing, or survival gear, it is plausible that she succumbed to the elements.

2. Foul Play: Initially, there were suspicions surrounding Susan's husband, Tom, and other members of the hunting party. However, all individuals involved

passed polygraph tests, and no evidence of foul play was found. Some speculated that the last person to see Susan alive, the chef at the base camp, might have been involved, but there was no evidence to support this.

3. Wild Animal Attack: The possibility of a wild animal attack, such as by a mountain lion, was considered. However, no signs of a struggle, blood, or torn clothing were found, making this scenario less likely.

4. Voluntary Disappearance: Some have speculated that Susan might have chosen to disappear voluntarily, but there is no evidence to support this theory. She was reported to be enjoying the trip and had made no indications of wanting to leave her life behind.

5. Supernatural or Unexplained Phenomena: As with many unsolved disappearances, some have suggested more outlandish theories involving supernatural or unexplained phenomena. While these theories capture the imagination, they are not grounded in evidence.

Susan's disappearance had a profound impact on her family and friends. Her husband, Tom, was deeply affected, and the lack of closure has been a constant source of pain. The case also highlighted the dangers of wilderness areas and the importance of being prepared when venturing into such environments.

The mystery of Susan Adams' disappearance continues to intrigue and baffle. Each year, new theories and occasional sightings are reported, but none have led to conclusive evidence. The case remains open, and authorities urge anyone with information to come forward.

The lack of closure has left a lasting impact on her loved ones, and the case continues to be a topic of interest for those fascinated by unexplained disappearances. As time goes on, the hope of finding answers persists, driven by the enduring love and determination of those who knew and cared for Susan.

# THIRTEEN

## THELMA PAULINE MELTON

THE DISAPPEARANCE of Thelma Pauline Melton, often referred to as "Polly," is one of the most perplexing cases in the history of the Great Smoky Mountains

National Park. On September 25, 1981, Polly, a 58-year-old woman from Jacksonville, Florida, vanished without a trace while hiking on a familiar trail.

———

Polly Melton was born on February 26, 1923, in Alabama. Described as friendly, intelligent, and generous, Polly was well-liked by those who knew her. She had a strong connection to the Great Smoky Mountains, spending nearly 20 years visiting the area regularly. She and her husband, Bob Melton, owned an Airstream trailer, which they parked at the Deep Creek Campground during their stays in the park.

Polly had several health issues, including high blood pressure and nausea, for which she took medication. Despite these conditions, she was active and enjoyed hiking the trails of the Smokies.

On the afternoon of September 25, 1981, Polly set out for a hike on the Deep Creek Trail with two friends, Red and Trula. The trail was one she knew well, having hiked it numerous times before. The group began their hike at around 3:00 PM. According to her friends, Polly seemed to be in good spirits as they walked along the trail.

As the group made their way back to the campground, Polly picked up her pace and walked ahead of her companions. She was last seen by her friends at around 4:00 PM, cresting a small hill and disappearing from view. Assuming she had simply gone ahead to the campground, Red and Trula continued at their own pace.

When Red and Trula arrived at the campground around 4:30 PM, they found Bob Melton inside the trailer, but Polly was nowhere to be seen. Bob had not seen her since she left for the hike. The friends began searching the area where they had last seen Polly, but there was no sign of her.

Polly was reported missing to a park ranger at approximately 6:00 PM, two hours after she was last seen. A large search operation was quickly launched, involving over 150 people, including park rangers, volunteers, and nine search dogs. Despite the extensive search, no trace of Polly was found.

One of the search dogs briefly alerted to a downed tree, suggesting that Polly might have stopped to rest there, but no further scent was detected. The searchers scoured the trail and surrounding areas, but there were no indications that anyone had ventured off the path.

Several eyewitness accounts and police details have added layers of mystery to Polly's disappearance. According to her friends, Polly was a large woman, standing 5'11" and weighing around 180 pounds. Given her size and the fact that she disappeared in broad daylight, authorities initially dismissed the possibility of an abduction, especially since no one had reported seeing anything suspicious.

Polly's medical conditions also played a role in the

investigation. She did not have her medication, identification, or any money with her when she vanished, carrying only a pack of cigarettes. Her husband mentioned that Polly had recently stopped taking Valium, which she had used as a muscle relaxant in the past. However, Bob discovered that his own bottle of Valium was missing after Polly disappeared, raising questions about whether she had taken the pills with her.

Another intriguing detail is that Polly had decided against volunteering at a senior citizen center where she usually served meals. On the day before her disappearance, she made an unusual phone call from the center's phone, which she had never used before in her four years of volunteering there. The recipient of the call remains unknown, and it is unclear whether it had any connection to her disappearance.

Over the years, several theories have been proposed to explain Polly's mysterious disappearance:

1. Medical Emergency: One possibility is that Polly suffered a medical emergency, such as a stroke or heart attack, which caused her to collapse and become lost or incapacitated. However, the extensive search efforts failed to locate her body, making this theory less likely.

2. Voluntary Disappearance: Some have speculated that Polly might have chosen to disappear voluntarily. She had been grieving the recent death of her mother and was reportedly struggling with depression. There

were also unsubstantiated rumors that she might have been having an affair. However, those who knew Polly described her as happy and well-adjusted, with no discernible reason to leave her life behind.

3. Abduction: Despite initial dismissals, the possibility of abduction cannot be entirely ruled out. Polly's friends noted that she disappeared very quickly, and there were no signs of a struggle. Given her size and the broad daylight setting, it would have been challenging for someone to abduct her without being noticed.

4. Accident: Another theory is that Polly might have accidentally fallen into a concealed area, such as a crevice or a hidden cave, where her body remains undiscovered. The Great Smoky Mountains are known for their rugged terrain, and it is possible that Polly met with an accident that took her out of sight.

5. Supernatural or Cryptid Encounter: Some fringe theories suggest that Polly might have encountered something supernatural or a cryptid, such as Bigfoot, which led to her disappearance. While these theories are far-fetched, they reflect the desperation and mystery surrounding her case.

---

The disappearance of Thelma Pauline Melton remains one of the most baffling cases in the history of the Great Smoky Mountains National Park. Despite extensive search efforts and numerous theories, no definitive answers have emerged to explain her sudden vanishing. As the years pass, the search for Polly continues, driven by the hope that someday, new evidence might come to light.

# FOURTEEN
STEFAN BISSERT

ON JANUARY 20, 1992, Stefan Bissert, a 23-year-old German exchange student and Fulbright scholar at Oregon State University, set off on a hike in the snow-covered mountains of Olympic National Park in Washington. What was meant to be a day of exploration turned into a baffling mystery when Stefan vanished without a trace.

———

Stefan Bissert was an ambitious and intelligent student from Bad Oeynhausen, Germany. He was studying physics at Oregon State University, making the most of his time in the United States by exploring its natural beauty. Stefan was described as adventurous yet cautious, traits that would later puzzle investigators trying to understand how he could have disappeared so completely.

On the morning of January 20, 1992, Stefan and a fellow German exchange student decided to hike in the Sol Duc area of Olympic National Park. The park, known for its dense forests, rugged terrain, and often unpredictable weather, can be both beautiful and treacherous.

The pair initially hiked together but eventually separated, with Stefan planning to hike the 23 miles from Sol Duc Hot Springs over High Divide to the Hoh River trailhead. This ambitious route would take him through some of the park's most remote and challenging areas. When Stefan failed to arrive at the predetermined meeting point, his friend reported him missing the next day.

The search for Stefan began immediately and involved a massive effort from park rangers, mountain rescue teams, and volunteers. Search dogs and helicopters were deployed to scour the area. Despite the intense search, which lasted several days, no trace of Stefan was found. The search was called off on January 27, 1992, due to the risk to the searchers and the diminishing likelihood of finding Stefan alive.

The difficult weather conditions, including snow and freezing temperatures, compounded the challenges faced by search teams. Stefan was not equipped for an overnight stay in such harsh conditions, which added to the urgency and ultimately the frustration of the search efforts.

Throughout the search, there were few clues to guide the investigators. No significant eyewitness accounts emerged that could provide a lead on Stefan's whereabouts. The park is vast and largely wilderness, making the task of finding someone particularly daunting if they are off the main trails.

One of the few tangible pieces of information came from Stefan's hiking partner, who confirmed that they had separated and that Stefan was planning to hike out alone. This decision, while not uncommon among experienced hikers, increased the difficulty of the search efforts as it left searchers with a large and varied area to cover without specific coordinates to focus on.

Several theories have been proposed to explain Stefan's disappearance, each reflecting the various hazards and possibilities inherent in wilderness hiking.

1. Accidental Fall: One of the most plausible theories is that Stefan may have fallen into one of the many ravines or crevices in the park. The terrain is rugged, and an unplanned slip or misstep could lead to a fatal fall, with the dense forest canopy potentially hiding his body from searchers above.

2. Exposure: Given the harsh winter conditions, it's possible that Stefan succumbed to hypothermia. Without proper gear, exposure to the elements could

have quickly become life-threatening. If he ventured off-trail or sought shelter in an obscure location, his body might have been missed during the search.

3. Animal Attack: While less likely, the possibility of an animal attack cannot be completely ruled out. Olympic National Park is home to black bears and mountain lions. An encounter with such wildlife, though rare, could result in a fatality.

4. Foul Play: Although there were no immediate signs of foul play, some have speculated that Stefan could have encountered someone with ill intentions. However, this theory lacks concrete evidence and is considered less likely by authorities.

5. Voluntary Disappearance: Some have speculated that Stefan might have chosen to disappear voluntarily. This theory is generally dismissed by those who knew him, citing his promising future and strong connections with family and friends.

Stefan's disappearance had a profound impact on his family and friends. His parents traveled from Germany to assist in the search and to be close to the efforts to find their son. The emotional toll on them was immense, as they grappled with the uncertainty and lack of closure.

The search for Stefan Bissert highlighted the risks associated with hiking in remote and challenging environments, particularly during winter. It also underscored the importance of being adequately prepared for sudden changes in weather and terrain conditions.

In the years following his disappearance, the case of Stefan Bissert has remained a topic of discussion among those familiar with the park's history of missing persons. Despite the extensive search efforts and the passage of time, Stefan's fate remains one of the enduring mysteries of Olympic National Park.

---

Despite the best efforts of search and rescue teams, some mysteries remain unsolved, leaving families and friends with unanswered questions and lingering hopes.

# CHAPTER
# FIFTEEN
CHET HANSON

CHET HANSON'S disappearance on November 11, 1997, remains one of the most perplexing cases in the history of Mount Rainier National Park. A 27-year-old photographer from Wilkeson, Washington, Chet was known for his adventurous spirit and love of nature. His sudden and unexplained disappearance has left investigators and his family searching for answers for over two decades.

———

On the morning of November 11, 1997, Chet Hanson set out for what was supposed to be a routine photography trip in Mount Rainier National Park. An employee of Alaska Airlines, Chet was an experienced hiker and photographer, often combining his two passions on solitary excursions into the wilderness. His destination that day was the Deer Creek Trailhead on Highway 123, a familiar spot he had visited numerous times before.

Chet was seen by several witnesses as he prepared for his hike. He was described as wearing hiking boots, a fleece jacket, and carrying a large-format camera and tripod. His plan was to photograph the winter landscape around Mount Rainier, a task he had undertaken many times before. However, he did not leave a detailed itinerary, a decision that would later complicate search efforts.

When Chet failed to report to work on November 12, his concerned colleagues notified his family, who in turn contacted the authorities. A search was initiated, and on November 14, 1997, Chet's vehicle was discovered at the Deer Creek Trailhead. Inside the car were several rolls of undeveloped film, a set of house keys, and his glasses, but no sign of Chet himself.

The discovery of his vehicle sparked a massive search operation. Park rangers, local law enforcement, and volunteers combed the area, using helicopters, search dogs, and ground teams to scour the trails and surrounding wilderness. Despite their efforts, no trace of Chet was found.

The initial search focused on the Deer Creek Trail and its surrounding areas. Given Chet's experience and familiarity with the terrain, search teams believed he might have ventured off the main path to capture unique photographic angles. Unfortunately, the rugged and heavily forested terrain made the search difficult and dangerous.

For over a week, search and rescue teams braved the cold November weather, hoping to find any sign of Chet. They followed every lead, including potential sightings and clues that might indicate his direction of travel. Despite their exhaustive efforts, the search was officially called off after ten days, leaving his family and friends in a state of despair and uncertainty.

During the search, several potential clues and eyewitness accounts emerged, though none provided a definitive answer. Some hikers reported seeing a man matching Chet's description near a secluded area known for its scenic views. Another witness claimed to have heard someone calling for help, but the sound was faint and could not be pinpointed.

One of the most intriguing clues was a set of footprints leading off the main trail. These prints matched the type of boots Chet was known to wear and seemed to head towards a remote part of the park. Search teams followed the prints for several miles before they abruptly ended near a steep and dangerous ravine. Despite a thorough investigation of the area, no further evidence was found.

Chet Hanson's disappearance has given rise to numerous theories, each attempting to explain what might have happened to him. The lack of concrete evidence has fueled speculation and intrigue, with several prominent theories standing out.

- Accidental Fall: One of the most plausible theories is that Chet may have fallen while attempting to capture a photograph in a precarious location. The abrupt end of his footprints near a ravine supports this theory. Given the rugged terrain and the possibility of snow or ice, it's conceivable that he lost his footing and fell, possibly becoming injured or trapped in a location that was not easily visible to search teams.
- Animal Attack: While less likely, the possibility of an animal attack has been considered.

Mount Rainier is home to a variety of wildlife, including bears and mountain lions. However, search teams found no signs of a struggle, blood, or other evidence that would typically accompany such an incident. The lack of physical evidence makes this theory less compelling.

- Voluntary Disappearance: Some have speculated that Chet may have chosen to disappear voluntarily. This theory is often considered in missing person cases where no clear evidence of foul play or accident is found. However, those who knew Chet well have dismissed this idea, citing his close relationships with family and friends and his plans for the future. There was no indication that he was unhappy or planning to start a new life elsewhere.

- Foul Play: The theory of foul play cannot be entirely ruled out, though there is no direct evidence to support it. The remote and isolated nature of the area makes it an unlikely spot for a random act of violence. However, some believe that Chet might have encountered someone with ill intentions during his hike. The lack of any personal items or signs of struggle near his vehicle makes this theory difficult to prove.

As the years have passed, Chet Hanson's disappearance has remained an open case. His family continues to search for answers, holding out hope that new evidence or a breakthrough might one day provide closure. They have kept his memory alive through various efforts, including setting up a website and social media pages dedicated to finding Chet and raising awareness about his case.

In the years following his disappearance, several individuals have come forward with potential leads and sightings. Each piece of information is meticulously investigated, though none have led to a definitive conclusion. The case has also been featured in several true crime podcasts and television shows, bringing renewed attention and occasionally generating new tips and theories.

———

Despite extensive search efforts, numerous eyewitness accounts, and countless theories, the truth about what happened to Chet on that fateful day in November 1997 continues to elude investigators and his loved ones. As new technologies and methodologies in search and rescue operations evolve, there remains a glimmer of hope that one day, the mystery of Chet Hanson's disappearance will be solved.

# CHAPTER
# SIXTEEN

## CONNIE JOHNSON

IN EARLY OCTOBER 2018, Connie Marie Johnson, a 76-year-old former U.S. Forest Service ranger and an experienced outdoorswoman, vanished without a trace from a remote hunting camp near Big Fog Mountain in Idaho.

———

Connie Johnson had spent much of her life in the wilderness. She worked for years as a wilderness ranger for the U.S. Forest Service and later as a guide for youth explorer programs. At the time of her disappearance, she was employed as a camp cook for Richie Outfitters, an organization that conducts hunting trips in the Montana and Idaho wilderness. Known for her deep knowledge of the outdoors, Connie was not someone who would easily get lost or be unprepared for the challenges of wilderness life.

Connie was last seen on October 2, 2018, at the hunting camp near Big Fog Mountain. She was with her dog, Ace, when the hunters left for a day and night trip. The next day, the hunters had brief radio contact with Connie, but the signal was weak, and they could not understand her message. This would be the last communication anyone had with her.

When the hunters returned to camp on October 5, 2018, they found it deserted. Connie and Ace were missing, but her coat and gun were left behind. The hunters immediately reported her disappearance to the authorities.

The search for Connie Johnson was extensive. Over three weeks, search teams combed hundreds of square miles using a combination of human searchers, canine units, helicopters equipped with FLIR (Forward Looking

Infrared) technology, and even a Forest Service plane. Despite these efforts, no trace of Connie was found. The official search was called off on October 16, 2018.

Three weeks after the search was halted, Ace, Connie's dog, was found near the Moose Creek ranger station, about fifteen miles from the camp. Ace was underweight but in good health. The searchers hoped that Ace might lead them to Connie, but the dog did not show any interest in retracing his steps or indicating where he had been.

Several theories have been proposed to explain Connie Johnson's disappearance, each drawing on different pieces of evidence and speculation:

- Accident or Medical Emergency: One of the most plausible theories is that Connie suffered an accident or medical emergency while alone in the wilderness. Given her age, it's possible she fell or had a sudden health issue that incapacitated her. The radio contact the day after the hunters left might have been an attempt to call for help, but the weak signal prevented effective communication.
- Environmental Factors: The remote and rugged terrain around Big Fog Mountain is challenging, even for an experienced outdoorswoman like Connie. Weather conditions can change rapidly in this area, and

it's possible that she was caught in a sudden storm or other environmental hazard.

- Animal Attack: While less likely given the lack of evidence, an animal attack cannot be entirely ruled out. However, no signs of a struggle or remains were found, making this scenario less probable.

- Foul Play: Although there is no concrete evidence to suggest foul play, some have speculated that Connie could have encountered another person with malicious intent. This theory is supported by the absence of any clues typically left behind in an accidental death scenario.

- Intentional Disappearance: Some have proposed that Connie might have chosen to disappear intentionally. However, those who knew her well, including her daughter, strongly dispute this idea, noting that Connie loved the outdoors and had no reason to vanish willingly.

- Coincidence with Other Disappearances: Intriguingly, another person, Terrence Woods, a production assistant, went missing in the same area around the same time. While it is unlikely that the two cases are connected, the coincidence has added another layer of mystery to Connie's disappearance.

The Idaho County Sheriff's Office led the investigation into Connie Johnson's disappearance. Despite the extensive search and rescue operation, no significant leads were found. The involvement of multiple agencies, including the Forest Service and volunteer search teams, highlighted the challenges of searching in such a vast and remote area.

Connie's family and friends have continued their efforts to find her, maintaining hope that new information might come to light. They have kept her story alive through media appearances and have sought help from private investigators. The discovery of Ace, while offering some hope, ultimately did not lead to any breakthroughs in the case.

———

The disappearance of Connie Johnson remains a perplexing mysteriy. Despite her extensive experience and knowledge of the outdoors, she vanished without a trace, leaving behind a series of unanswered questions and unresolved theories. Her family and friends continue to seek closure, holding onto the hope that someday they will find out what happened to their beloved Connie.

ON A FATEFUL DAY in July 2013, 66-year-old Geraldine "Gerry" Largay, an experienced hiker, vanished while traversing the Appalachian Trail in Maine. Her disappearance sparked the largest search-

and-rescue operation in Maine's history and captured the nation's attention.

----

Gerry Largay was a retired nurse from Tennessee with a passion for hiking. Her trail name, "Inchworm," reflected her steady, determined pace. Gerry and her husband, George, planned for her to hike the Appalachian Trail, with George meeting her periodically for resupply and moral support. Initially, Gerry hiked with her friend Jane Lee, but Jane had to leave the hike due to a family emergency just as they entered the challenging terrain of Maine's White Mountains.

On July 22, 2013, Gerry left the Poplar Ridge Lean-to and hiked north. She was last seen by fellow hikers Dottie Rust and Regina Clark, who described her as confident and cheerful. Gerry planned to meet George at the Route 27 crossing two days later. However, she never arrived.

Gerry stepped off the trail to relieve herself and became disoriented. At 11:01 AM, she tried to send a text message to George: "In somm trouble. Got off trail to go to br. Now lost." Unfortunately, due to the lack of cell service, the message never sent. Desperate, she attempted to find higher ground to get a signal but ultimately became more lost. Over the next few days, she tried several more times to text her husband, all to no avail.

When Gerry failed to meet George, he reported her missing, triggering an extensive search operation involving the Maine Warden Service, volunteers, and even the Navy. Searchers scoured the Appalachian Trail and surrounding areas but found no trace of Gerry. The dense forest, challenging terrain, and lack of initial clues hampered the search efforts.

On October 14, 2015, surveyors conducting routine work stumbled upon Gerry's campsite in Redington Township, about 3,000 feet from the trail. Her remains were found inside her tent, along with her journal, which detailed her final days. The journal revealed that Gerry survived for at least 26 days, rationing her food and attempting to signal for help.

Eyewitnesses provided critical information that helped piece together Gerry's last known movements. Rust and Clark, the last hikers to see her, noted that Gerry seemed in good spirits and well-prepared for the hike. However, other hikers on the trail and search teams failed to find any signs of her after she went missing.

Several theories have emerged to explain Gerry's disappearance:

- Disorientation and Navigation Errors: Gerry's initial decision to leave the trail to relieve herself, combined with the dense forest and lack of visible markers, likely led to her becoming disoriented. Without a map or compass, finding her way back to the trail proved impossible.

- Survival Challenges: Despite being an experienced hiker, Gerry was not a trained survivalist. Her journal entries indicated she was aware of her dire situation and attempted to survive by rationing food and conserving energy. However, without adequate supplies and with no rescue in sight, her situation became untenable.

- Communication Failures: The lack of cell service in the remote area prevented Gerry's distress messages from reaching her husband. This failure underscores the challenges hikers face in maintaining communication in wilderness areas. Modern technologies like satellite phones or personal locator beacons could have significantly increased her chances of rescue.

Gerry's tragic story has led to increased awareness and changes in hiking safety practices. Hikers are now more encouraged to carry reliable navigation tools and communication devices. Her story has been documented in books and articles, serving as a sobering reminder of the wilderness's dangers and the importance of preparation.

————

Geraldine "Gerry" Largay's disappearance and the subsequent discovery of her remains highlight the perils of solo hiking in remote areas. Despite her experience and determination, a series of unfortunate events led to her tragic end. The exhaustive search efforts and the poignant details of her final days, as recorded in her journal, provide a powerful narrative of human resilience and the unforgiving nature of the wild. Her legacy continues to influence hiking safety and serves as a cautionary tale for all who venture into the wilderness.

# CHAPTER
# EIGHTEEN

MICHAEL HEARON

MICHAEL EDWIN HEARON, a successful builder
and devoted father, disappeared under baffling circumstances on August 23, 2008. His case remains one of the

most perplexing unsolved mysteries in Tennessee, capti-
vating the public's attention and drawing significant
media coverage.

————

Michael Hearon, commonly known as Mike, was a 51-
year-old man from Maryville, Tennessee. He was known
for his love of the outdoors, frequently working on his
hundred-acre property in Happy Valley, near the Great
Smoky Mountains National Park. A former park service
employee who founded a successful home construction
business, Mike was well-regarded in his community and
had a close relationship with his two sons, Matt and
Andy.

On the morning of August 23, 2008, Mike left his
condo in Maryville and drove to his property in Happy
Valley. He called his sons to inform them of his plans, as
there was no cell phone service on the farm, and he often
worked out of earshot of the house phone. He intended
to spend the day mowing his fields, a routine task he had
performed countless times before.

Mike was last seen by neighbors around 11:00 AM,
riding his green Yamaha Wolverine ATV. He waved to
them as he passed, seemingly in good spirits. However,
this would be the last confirmed sighting of him. Later
that day, Mike's truck was found parked unusually at the

end of his driveway, with the trailer still attached and the mower on it. His personal belongings, including his keys, wallet, cell phone, money clip, and gun, were inside the truck, which had its windows rolled down.

When Mike's sons and ex-wife arrived at the farm on August 24 and found his truck still parked at the end of the road, they began to worry. By the afternoon of August 25, after searching the property themselves, they reported him missing to the authorities. The Blount County Sheriff's Office, along with the National Park Service, initiated a search that evening, despite heavy rains that hampered efforts.

The search involved extensive ground efforts, including ATVs, horses, and sniffer dogs, but no trace of Mike was found. His ATV was discovered on August 26, abandoned in an area he rarely visited, near an abandoned cabin close to the National Park. The ATV was found in high gear with the ignition switch on and the kill switch off, which was unusual for Mike, as he would never leave the ATV in such a state.

One of the most intriguing aspects of Mike's disappearance is the lack of physical evidence. Despite the extensive search efforts, no footprints, broken vegetation, or other signs indicated where Mike might have gone. His neighbors, who had seen him riding the ATV, reported nothing unusual, and there were no signs of a struggle or accident near the ATV's location.

The fact that the ATV was found in high gear and with the ignition on led Mike's sons to believe foul play was involved. They noted that Mike, an experienced outdoorsman, would never have left his vehicle in such a condition unless something unexpected had happened. The ATV's location also raised suspicions, as it was found on a steep hill in dense brush, far from where Mike usually traveled.

Over the years, several theories have been proposed to explain Mike's disappearance:

- Accident: Initially, some speculated that Mike might have had an accident and was injured or incapacitated somewhere in the vast wilderness. However, the lack of any physical evidence or signs of an accident at the scene makes this theory less plausible.
- Foul Play: Many, including Mike's family, believe he encountered foul play. Given the unusual state of the ATV and the absence of any other clues, it is possible that Mike stumbled upon illegal activities, such as drug operations or poaching, and was subsequently harmed to prevent him from reporting what he saw.
- Voluntary Disappearance: While some consider the possibility that Mike chose to disappear voluntarily, those who knew him

well find this unlikely. He had no history of mental health issues, was not experiencing significant personal problems, and had plans for the future, including spending time with his newly married sons and potential grandchildren.

- Animal Attack: Another theory suggests that Mike might have been attacked by a wild animal. However, this theory is also deemed improbable due to the lack of evidence such as blood or torn clothing at the scene where the ATV was found.

The Blount County Sheriff's Office has kept Mike's case open, but there have been no significant leads in recent years. The community continues to be haunted by his disappearance, with many still hoping for closure. Despite the lack of progress, the Hearon family and law enforcement remain vigilant, encouraging anyone with information to come forward.

In 2021, a podcast episode dedicated to Mike's case renewed public interest, highlighting the various aspects and unresolved questions surrounding his disappearance. This has led to some renewed efforts in the investigation, but as of now, no new evidence has surfaced.

———

Michael Hearon's disappearance remains an unsolved mystery, leaving his family and community in a state of perpetual uncertainty. As the years pass, the hope for answers persists, driven by the enduring love and determination of Mike's family.

# NINETEEN
KRIS FOWLER

KRIS FOWLER, known by his trail name "Sherpa," was an experienced hiker who embarked on the Pacific Crest Trail (PCT) in 2016. His journey was meant to be a testament to his love for the outdoors and his adventurous spirit. However, his hike ended in tragedy when he disappeared without a trace in Washington State.

———

Kris Fowler was a 34-year-old avid hiker and disc golf player from Ohio. He decided to hike the PCT, a 2,650-mile trail stretching from Mexico to Canada, as a way to see more of the country and challenge himself physically and mentally. Fowler began his hike on May 8, 2016, with his friend Colin Hurley. Although they started together, they soon parted ways, each hiking at their own pace. Fowler, who enjoyed photography, often took longer on the trail to capture unique moments and scenes.

On October 12, 2016, Fowler was last seen at White Pass, Washington, at mile 2,294 of the PCT. He was reportedly seen at a Cracker Barrel store, where he stopped to get coffee before heading back to the trail. That evening, his cell phone pinged for the last time near White Pass, around 5:43 PM. The area was expecting considerable amounts of snow and rain over the following days, raising concerns about his safety.

When Kris failed to check in with his family as planned, his stepmother, Sally Guyton Fowler, and his father, Mike, grew increasingly worried. By October 23, 2016, it became clear that Kris was missing. Despite the family's initial struggle to convince authorities of the seriousness of the situation, a large-scale search was eventually launched. This included a five-county search effort that spanned two weeks but was hampered by inclement weather.

The search involved various agencies and volunteers, including the Yakima County Sheriff's Office and Kittitas County search and rescue teams. Retired Yakima County Sgt. Randy Briscoe played a significant role in coordinating the search efforts, which included ground searches, aerial surveys, and the use of search dogs. Despite these extensive efforts, no trace of Kris was found.

Throughout the investigation, several potential leads surfaced, though none provided conclusive evidence. In one instance, a hiker reported seeing what looked like Kris's tent, but upon investigation, it turned out to be two abandoned tents stacked on top of each other. Such leads, while disappointing, underscore the difficulty and complexity of searching in rugged wilderness areas.

Kris was known to be in contact with other hikers, and some reported communicating with him shortly before his disappearance. For instance, he had texted a fellow hiker on October 12, mentioning issues with his phone charger. These communications were critical in piecing together his last known movements but ultimately did not lead to his whereabouts.

Numerous theories have emerged regarding Kris

Fowler's disappearance, reflecting the myriad possibilities and the uncertainty surrounding his fate.

- Adverse Weather Conditions: The most plausible theory is that Kris was caught in severe weather conditions. Snow and rain were expected in the area, which could have led to hypothermia or disorientation. This theory is supported by the timing of his last known movements and the environmental conditions reported at the time.
- Accidental Fall or Injury: Another theory posits that Kris might have suffered an accidental fall or injury while hiking. The PCT in Washington State is known for its challenging terrain, and it's possible he ventured off the main trail to explore or take photographs, leading to an accident.
- Wildlife Encounter: Encounters with wildlife, such as bears or mountain lions, are not uncommon in the area. While less likely, this remains a consideration given the remote and wild nature of the trail.
- Foul Play: Although there's no evidence to support this, some have speculated about the possibility of foul play. This theory is less favored given the lack of any suspicious

findings or evidence pointing to criminal activity.

- Voluntary Disappearance: A less likely but still considered theory is that Kris might have chosen to disappear voluntarily. However, his close relationship with his family and friends, and his consistent check-ins throughout his journey, make this unlikely.

The search for Kris Fowler has continued long after the initial efforts ceased. His family, particularly his stepmother, Sally, has been relentless in seeking answers. They have engaged with numerous volunteer groups and organizations, including the Fowler-O'Sullivan Foundation, which was established to assist families of missing hikers. The foundation, named after Kris and another missing hiker, David O'Sullivan, provides resources and support for search efforts and raises awareness about missing persons on trails.

Volunteers like Cathy Tarr have dedicated significant time and resources to finding Kris and other missing hikers. These efforts include organizing search parties, distributing flyers, and maintaining an online presence to keep the public informed and engaged. The hope is that continued awareness will lead to new information or discoveries that could solve the mystery of Kris's disappearance.

———

The disappearance of Kris Fowler remains a haunting mystery on the Pacific Crest Trail. Despite extensive searches and the tireless efforts of his family and volunteers, no conclusive evidence has emerged to explain what happened to him. As the years pass, his family and friends continue to search, driven by the belief that one day, they will uncover the truth of what happened to their beloved Sherpa on that fateful October day in 2016.

# CHAPTER
# TWENTY

GILBERT "GIL" MARK GILMAN

ON JUNE 24, 2006, GILBERT "GIL" Mark Gilman, a 47-year-old former military interrogator and deputy director of the Washington State Pension Fund, vanished without a trace during a day hike in the Olympic National Park, Washington. Despite his extensive training and experience, his disappearance remains a mystery, leaving behind a trail of speculation and unanswered questions.

———

Gilbert Gilman was a seasoned veteran, having served as an Army paratrooper and military interrogator. He held positions in counter-terrorism and counter-intelligence, and worked with the United Nations. Fluent in multiple languages, including Arabic, Russian, and Chinese, Gilman had a diverse and accomplished career. He had recently moved from New York to Washington State and was known for his love of the outdoors, making his disappearance during a hike all the more puzzling.

On June 24, 2006, Gilman set out for a hike on the Staircase Rapids Loop Trail in the Olympic National Park. This trail is relatively short and well-marked, typically taking about two hours to complete. Gilman was last seen at the Staircase Ranger Station, where he parked his silver 2005 Ford Thunderbird. He was dressed in a bright blue and green Hawaiian shirt, khaki pants or shorts, sandals, and prescription sunglasses, carrying only a camera.

When Gilman failed to meet a coworker for a scheduled business trip to Spokane the following day, concern grew. His coworker reported him missing on June 25. Authorities discovered his car at the ranger station, suggesting it had been there since the day he was last seen.

The search for Gilman was extensive. Over ten days, 62 searchers scoured the area, assisted by tracking dogs, a helicopter, and a small plane equipped with heat-seeking technology. Despite these efforts, no trace of Gilman was found. The search area included steep, rocky hills, dense forests, and the North Fork Skokomish River, making the terrain challenging.

Gilman's military background and survival skills added a layer of complexity to the search. He was in good health and had experience in harsh conditions. However, the fact that he did not take a backpack or other supplies indicated he did not plan to be out for long. His nearsightedness without his glasses further complicated theories about his fate.

Several theories have been proposed to explain Gilman's disappearance:

- Accidental Death: Given the rugged terrain, it's possible Gilman had an accident and succumbed to the elements. However, the lack of any physical evidence, such as clothing or belongings, casts doubt on this theory.
- Intentional Disappearance*: Some believe Gilman may have chosen to disappear. His mother speculated he could have taken up a covert assignment, potentially as a spy for the

U.S. government, given his background in intelligence. This theory suggests he might have staged his disappearance to start a new life or fulfill a secret mission. However, there is no concrete evidence to support this.

- Foul Play: Another theory involves foul play. In 2014, an episode of the television show "Dark Minds" linked Gilman's disappearance to Israel Keyes, a known serial killer. Keyes, an avid hiker who lived in the area and had access to the park, was known for disposing of his victims in remote locations. Although Keyes committed suicide in 2012 and admitted to several murders, the FBI found no direct evidence linking him to Gilman's case.

- Lost in the Wilderness: Despite the trail being well-marked, it's possible Gilman ventured off the path and got lost. The dense forest and challenging terrain could have made it difficult for search teams to locate him. This theory aligns with the idea that he may have become disoriented or injured, leading to his inability to return or signal for help.

Several unresolved questions continue to haunt investigators and Gilman's family:

- Why was there no trace of him found despite extensive search efforts? The search covered a significant area with no evidence discovered, raising questions about the thoroughness and timing of the search.
- What role, if any, did Gilman's background in military intelligence play in his disappearance? His career and language skills point to possible involvement in sensitive operations, but no official confirmation exists.
- Could Israel Keyes have been involved? While intriguing, the lack of evidence makes this theory speculative.

———

The disappearance of Gilbert "Gil" Mark Gilman remains one of the most baffling cases in recent history. Despite exhaustive search efforts, numerous theories, and the passage of time, no definitive answers have emerged. As his family continues to seek closure, the hope remains that one day, the mystery of Gilman's disappearance will be solved, bringing answers to those who have been left in the dark for so long.

# CHAPTER
# TWENTY-ONE

BRYAN LEE JOHNSTON

ON AUGUST 22, 2013, Bryan Lee Johnston, a 71-year-old hiker from Seattle, Washington, set off on a planned two- to three-day hike on the Ozette Loop Trail in Olympic National Park. Johnston, an experienced outdoorsman known for his meticulous nature and physical fitness, never returned from this trip, sparking a massive search effort and leaving his family in a state of ongoing anguish and uncertainty.

––––––

Bryan Lee Johnston was described as a fit and active 71-year-old who enjoyed hiking, photography, and various outdoor activities. He was known for his careful planning and extensive knowledge of the outdoors, traits that made his disappearance even more baffling to those who knew him. Johnston had served in the Air Force, worked for Seattle City Light as an engineer, and was deeply involved in his family and community life. His wife, Susan, and his stepchildren were deeply concerned when he did not return as planned from his hiking trip.

On the evening of August 21, 2013, Johnston informed his family of his plans to hike the Ozette Loop Trail, a popular nine-mile trail in Olympic National Park. He left a note for his sleeping wife early the next morning and took the Edmonds-Kingston ferry to the Olympic Peninsula. The last known sightings of Johnston include a cashier at a Safeway store in Port Angeles and a waitress at Traylor's Restaurant, both of whom saw him purchasing supplies for his hike.

Johnston's family reported him missing on August 28, after he failed to return and they found his truck parked at the Ozette trailhead. Inside the truck, park rangers discovered receipts from Port Angeles businesses dated August 22, the day he left home, but no further clues.

Upon receiving the report of Johnston's disappearance, more than 50 park rangers and volunteer search teams from Clallam, Grays Harbor, and Pierce counties were mobilized to search the Ozette Loop Trail and surrounding areas. The initial search included ground teams, boat teams, and search dogs, covering the trail, its surroundings, and the Pacific Coast shoreline extensively.

Despite these efforts, no sign of Johnston was found. The search was intensified with additional dog teams and ground searchers, but still, no clues emerged. Searchers distributed flyers with Johnston's photograph and description, interviewed hikers, and reviewed surveillance footage from the locations where he was last seen.

The last confirmed sightings of Johnston were in Port Angeles on August 22. The surveillance tape from Safeway showed him purchasing a sandwich, fruit, and water bottles. A waitress at Traylor's Restaurant also recalled serving him, but these accounts did not provide any insight into what might have happened on the trail.

In 2017, a hiker found one of Johnston's boots on the Ozette Loop Trail and turned it over to the authorities. This discovery, however, did not lead to any further evidence or explanation of Johnston's fate.

Several theories have been proposed regarding Johnston's disappearance, each with its own set of speculations and unanswered questions.

- Natural Causes or Accidental Injury: Given Johnston's age, some speculate that he may have suffered a medical emergency or accidental injury that left him incapacitated. The rugged terrain of the Ozette Loop Trail, particularly the coastal section, presents numerous hazards that could lead to a fall or other injury. However, the extensive search did not uncover any evidence to support this theory.
- Getting Lost: While the plank trails of the Ozette Loop are generally well-marked and hard to lose, the beach portion of the hike could be more challenging, especially during high tides. It's possible that Johnston ventured off the main trail, but his experience and meticulous nature make this seem unlikely.
- Intentional Disappearance: Some suggest that Johnston may have chosen to disappear voluntarily. However, his family strongly disputes this idea, citing his close relationships and his enthusiastic plans for the future.
- Foul Play: Although there is no evidence pointing to foul play, some cannot dismiss the possibility entirely. The remote nature of the

trail and the lack of witnesses leave room for speculation about an encounter that could have led to Johnston's disappearance.

- Supernatural or Unexplained Phenomena: In the absence of concrete evidence, some have even speculated about supernatural causes or unexplained phenomena. Johnston's sister, Jinny Longfellow, mentioned that a paranormal researcher suggested UFO involvement, though this remains purely speculative and not taken seriously by the investigation.

Johnston's disappearance has had a profound impact on his family and the local community. His wife, Susan Johnston, has remained hopeful, expressing her belief that Bryan is still alive and awaiting discovery. She continues to advocate for ongoing search efforts and keeps the public engaged through social media and news outlets.

Jinny Longfellow, Johnston's sister, holds on to the hope that her brother is still alive and possibly unaware that people are looking for him. She recounts their close relationship and shared adventures, describing him as a caring and resourceful person who would not simply vanish without a trace.

Despite the passage of time, the search for Bryan Lee Johnston has not been entirely abandoned. Park rangers and volunteers remain vigilant, and Johnston's family continues to seek answers. The case is periodically revisited by search teams, and new information is always welcomed.

———

As his family continues to hope for answers, the search for truth and resolution continues, fueled by the love and determination of those who knew him best.

# CHAPTER
# TWENTY-TWO
DAVID O'SULLIVAN

DAVID O'SULLIVAN, a 25-year-old Irish hiker, disappeared in April 2017 while attempting to thru-hike the Pacific Crest Trail (PCT), a 2,653-mile trail stretching from Mexico to Canada.

———

David O'Sullivan was born on August 29, 1991, in Cork, Ireland. He was a well-educated young man with a degree in English and Philosophy from University College Cork. An avid reader and lover of nature, David was inspired to hike the PCT after reading Cheryl Strayed's book "Wild." He meticulously planned his adventure, aiming to complete the trail in five to six months.

David began his hike on March 22, 2017, from Campo, California, near the Mexican border. His journey started smoothly, and he frequently updated his family via email. On April 6, he sent an email from a library in Idyllwild, California, a small mountain town. He planned to continue north into the San Jacinto Mountains the following day. This was the last confirmed contact from David.

David was reported missing when he failed to check in with his family as planned. The family reported his disappearance to the Irish police in late June, who then alerted the Riverside County Sheriff's Department. Initial searches were delayed, complicating the efforts to locate him.

On April 7, 2017, David checked out of the Idyllwild Inn and presumably headed back to the trail. Weather conditions were reportedly good, but a snowstorm hit the area shortly after, raising concerns about his safety. Multiple trails lead from Idyllwild to the PCT, but it remains unclear which one David took.

Search efforts for David O'Sullivan have been extensive and ongoing. Volunteers, including members of San Diego's Irish community, have scoured the mountains on foot and horseback. Drones have been deployed to cover large areas, capturing thousands of images for analysis. An aerial survey in December 2017 over Idyllwild utilized advanced photography and software to search for any trace of David's blue backpack or other belongings, but no definitive evidence was found.

Several hikers reported seeing David between April 10 and April 15 at a trail angel's house near Cabazon, north of San Diego. Trail angels are individuals who assist hikers with food, shelter, and transportation. This sighting indicated that David continued his journey beyond Idyllwild, but the exact trail he followed remains unknown.

Theories about David's disappearance range from accidental death to foul play. The most likely scenario, given the timing of the snowstorm, is that David succumbed to the harsh weather conditions and possibly fell or became incapacitated. However, the possibility of foul play cannot be entirely ruled out, especially considering the vast and often treacherous terrain of the PCT.

David's family has made multiple trips to California, coordinating searches and raising awareness about his case. His mother, Carmel O'Sullivan, has been vocal about the importance of finding out what happened to her son. The family has faced numerous challenges, including the COVID-19 pandemic, which halted search operations in 2020. Despite these setbacks, they remain determined to uncover the truth.

Carmel described David as a careful and experienced hiker, making his disappearance all the more perplexing. The family holds on to the hope of finding closure, whether it means bringing David home or understanding the circumstances of his fate.

In response to the disappearances of David O'Sullivan and other hikers like Kris Fowler, the Fowler-O'Sullivan Foundation was established. This organization assists families of missing hikers, advocating for better search and rescue efforts and providing support during the difficult search process. The foundation has been instrumental in organizing volunteer searches and utilizing technology to aid in the search for David and others.

————

The search for David continues, driven by the love and perseverance of his family and the support of the hiking community. As the years pass, the hope remains that someday, the mystery of his disappearance will be solved, bringing closure to his family and friends.

# TWENTY-THREE
## JOHN DONOVAN

JOHN DONOVAN, a seasoned hiker and lover of the great outdoors, disappeared in May 2005 while hiking the Pacific Crest Trail (PCT) in Southern California. His case remains one of the most intriguing and tragic mysteries within the hiking community.

———

John Donovan, at 59 years old, was an experienced hiker who had embarked on numerous long-distance hikes throughout his life. His passion for the wilderness and exploration was well-known among his friends and family. Donovan was described as a fit, resourceful, and resilient individual, making his disappearance all the more baffling.

Donovan set out on the Pacific Crest Trail in late April 2005. The PCT is a challenging 2,650-mile trail that spans from the Mexican border to Canada, traversing through California, Oregon, and Washington. Donovan planned to hike a section of the trail in Southern California, passing through the San Jacinto Mountains.

On May 2, 2005, Donovan was last seen by fellow hikers near the Fuller Ridge area of the San Jacinto Mountains. The region is known for its rugged terrain and unpredictable weather conditions. Donovan had informed friends and family of his route, and he was expected to make periodic contact during his hike. When days passed without any communication, concern began to grow.

The initial search for John Donovan was extensive. When he failed to make contact as planned, a large-scale search and rescue operation was launched. The search teams, consisting of experienced hikers, rescue person-nel, and even volunteers from the hiking community, combed the treacherous terrain of the San Jacinto Mountains.

Despite the considerable efforts, the search was hampered by the ruggedness of the area and severe weather conditions, including late spring snowstorms that swept through the mountains. The search continued for weeks, but no trace of Donovan was found. His disappearance remained a distressing enigma.

A year later, in May 2006, two hikers, Ray Nelson and Marlene Bunch, who themselves had become lost in the San Jacinto Mountains, stumbled upon a campsite. The site was located in a remote area far off the main trail. Among the items at the campsite were a tent, a sleeping bag, and various personal belongings, all of which appeared to have been abandoned for some time.

Further investigation by search and rescue teams confirmed that the belongings indeed belonged to John Donovan. The discovery rekindled hope of solving the mystery, and a renewed search effort was launched. This time, searchers focused on the area surrounding the campsite.

During this renewed search, human remains were discovered. While the remains were initially believed to be Donovan's, conclusive identification through DNA testing was necessary. The results confirmed that the remains were indeed those of John Donovan.

The circumstances surrounding John Donovan's death remained unclear. The location of his campsite suggested that he had veered significantly off the main trail. Various theories emerged to explain how an experienced hiker like Donovan could have become lost.

One theory posits that Donovan may have taken a wrong turn during adverse weather conditions. The late-season snowstorm that hit the region around the time of his disappearance could have obscured the trail, leading him off course. Another possibility is that he might have sustained an injury, rendering him unable to navigate back to the main trail.

The state of his campsite and the presence of his personal belongings indicated that he had set up a temporary shelter, possibly in hopes of being found or until he could figure out a way back to the trail. The exact cause of his death remains undetermined, but it is likely that exposure to the elements played a significant role.

During the initial search, several hikers reported having seen Donovan on the trail. These accounts were consistent with the known timeline of his hike up until May 2, 2005. After that date, there were no confirmed sightings of him. The hikers who last saw Donovan described him as being in good spirits and adequately equipped for his journey.

The hikers who discovered Donovan's campsite, Ray Nelson and Marlene Bunch, provided crucial information that helped to narrow down the search area. Their own ordeal of being lost in the mountains highlighted the dangers and challenges of the terrain, further under-scoring the perilous conditions Donovan might have faced.

Several theories have been proposed to explain the mysterious disappearance of John Donovan:

- Navigational Error: The most plausible theory is that Donovan lost his way due to poor visibility and treacherous weather conditions. Snow can obscure trail markers and create disorientation, even for seasoned hikers.
- Injury or Illness: It is possible that Donovan sustained an injury or fell ill, preventing him from continuing his hike. The remote location of his campsite suggests he may have been immobilized or unable to find his way back to the main trail.
- Wildlife Encounter: Although less likely, an encounter with wildlife cannot be entirely ruled out. However, there was no evidence of animal activity at his campsite that would suggest an attack.
- Intentional Disappearance: Some speculated that Donovan might have chosen to disappear intentionally. However, those who knew him well dismissed this idea, citing his love for his family and the outdoors, and his detailed planning of the hike.

- Foul Play: While there was no evidence to suggest foul play, it remains a consideration in any unsolved disappearance. However, the location of his remains and personal belongings did not indicate any struggle or foul play.

———

Despite his experience and preparedness, Donovan fell victim to the unpredictable and often unforgiving nature of the wilderness.

His case highlights the importance of caution, preparation, and the use of modern navigation tools while hiking in remote areas. The hiking community continues to remember John Donovan, not only for the mystery surrounding his disappearance but also for his enduring spirit of adventure.

The investigation into his death remains open, as authorities seek to fully understand the circumstances that led to his demise. The lessons learned from his case continue to inform and guide search and rescue operations in similar situations, underscoring the need for vigilance and safety in the great outdoors.

# CHAPTER
# TWENTY-FOUR

DEORR KUNZ, JR

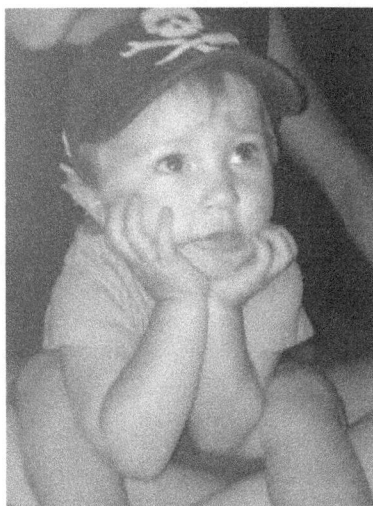

THE DISAPPEARANCE of DeOrr Kunz Jr., a two-year-old boy who vanished without a trace during a family camping trip in Idaho, has captivated and confounded both the public and investigators since it occurred in July 2015. The case is shrouded in mystery, with inconsistent statements from key figures and a multitude of theories, ranging from accidental death to foul play.

———

On July 9, 2015, DeOrr Kunz Jr. embarked on a camping trip to Timber Creek Campground, located in the remote wilderness of Lemhi County, Idaho. Accompanying him were his parents, Jessica Mitchell and Vernal DeOrr Kunz Sr., his great-grandfather Robert Walton, and Walton's friend Isaac Reinwand. The campsite, about a two-and-a-half-hour drive from Idaho Falls, is situated in a rugged, mountainous area known for its natural beauty and isolation.

The timeline of events on July 10, 2015, the day DeOrr went missing, is crucial to understanding the case. According to Jessica and Vernal, they, along with DeOrr Jr., visited a nearby general store that morning to buy snacks and supplies. They returned to the campsite, where DeOrr was reportedly left in the care of his great-grandfather while his parents went to explore a nearby creek for potential fishing spots.

DeOrr's parents claimed they were gone for about 10 to 15 minutes. When they returned, they found that their son was missing. They searched the immediate area for approximately 20 minutes before calling 911 at 2:28 PM to report DeOrr missing. This marked the beginning of an exhaustive search and investigation that has spanned years without yielding concrete answers.

Search and rescue teams, including local law enforcement, volunteers, and specialized units such as K9 teams and divers, were mobilized quickly. The initial search focused on a two-and-a-half-mile radius around the campsite. Despite extensive efforts over several days, including searches by air and on horseback, no trace of DeOrr was found. The search was particularly challenging due to the dense terrain and numerous waterways in the area.

Subsequent searches continued over the years, employing advanced technology such as drones and ATVs, yet these too failed to uncover any evidence of DeOrr's whereabouts. The lack of physical evidence has been a significant hurdle, leading to various theories and speculations.

Eyewitness accounts from those present at the campsite have been inconsistent, contributing to the complexity of the case. Great-grandfather Robert Walton initially stated he had never been with DeOrr, later changing his account to say he saw the boy near the creek before he disappeared. Walton's friend, Isaac Reinwand, provided a detailed timeline of the day but could not offer any clear insight into DeOrr's fate.

The most significant inconsistencies, however, have come from DeOrr's parents. Vernal Kunz and Jessica

Mitchell have been interviewed multiple times, and their stories have varied with each retelling. This has led law enforcement to consider them persons of interest in the case. Lemhi County Sheriff Lynn Bowerman has publicly expressed doubts about the parents' accounts, stating, "Mom and dad are being less than truthful. Every time we speak with them, parts of their story change."

The disappearance of DeOrr Kunz Jr. has given rise to several theories, each with its own set of proponents and detractors. These theories include:

- Accidental Death: One theory posits that DeOrr may have wandered off and succumbed to the elements or fallen into one of the nearby creeks or reservoirs. However, extensive searches have failed to uncover any evidence to support this scenario.
- Animal Attack: Given the remote and wild nature of the campground, some speculate that DeOrr could have been attacked by a wild animal. Yet, no signs of such an attack, such as blood or clothing, were found during the search efforts.
- Abduction: Another theory is that DeOrr was abducted, either by someone at the campground or by an unknown party. This theory is complicated by the isolated location

and lack of credible witnesses who saw DeOrr being taken.

- Foul Play by Family Members: The most contentious theory suggests that DeOrr's parents or another family member might have been involved in his disappearance, either intentionally or accidentally. The parents' inconsistent statements, failed polygraph tests, and the fact that key items, such as the jacket DeOrr was allegedly wearing, were left behind when the parents moved out, have fueled suspicions.

The investigation into DeOrr's disappearance has seen multiple phases, with involvement from local law enforcement, the FBI, and private investigators. Early on, Philip Klein, a private investigator hired by the family, concluded that DeOrr's parents were likely responsible for their son's disappearance. Klein cited the parents' inconsistent stories and multiple failed polygraph tests as critical factors in his assessment. He eventually terminated his contract with the family, stating that he believed the parents knew more than they were admitting.

In January 2016, Vernal Kunz and Jessica Mitchell were officially named suspects by the Lemhi County Sheriff's Office. Despite this designation, no charges have been filed due to a lack of direct evidence. The case remains open and active, with periodic searches and reviews of the evidence continuing.

As of 2023, DeOrr Kunz Jr.'s case remains unsolved. The lack of resolution has been a source of ongoing anguish for DeOrr's family, particularly his grandmother, Trina Clegg, who continues to hope for answers. The case has also drawn significant media attention and public interest, with many amateur sleuths and true crime enthusiasts debating the various theories and potential outcomes.

Theories about DeOrr's fate range widely, reflecting the case's complexity and the emotional investment of those following it. Some believe that new evidence will eventually come to light, leading to a resolution, while others fear the case may never be solved.

———

The disappearance of DeOrr Kunz Jr. is a tragic and perplexing case. The case continues to evoke strong emotions and speculation, with many hoping that someday, the truth will be uncovered, providing closure to those who loved him and clarity to those who have followed his story.

# TWENTY-FIVE
ALEXANDER PISCH

ALEXANDER "ALEX" Pisch, a 35-year-old landscape painter from Discovery Bay, California, disappeared on October 8, 2020, near Colonial Creek Campground in North Cascades National Park, Washington.

———

Alex Pisch was known for his love of nature and his passion for painting landscapes. Friends and family described him as a talented artist who found inspiration in the tranquility of the outdoors. His decision to visit the North Cascades National Park was in line with his artistic pursuits, seeking to capture the natural beauty of the region on canvas.

On October 8, 2020, Pisch set out for a day of painting at a scenic spot along Diablo Lake. He was last seen setting up his easel near the Colonial Creek Campground, a popular area for campers and hikers. His white Toyota Corolla was found parked along Highway 20, with his painting supplies and easel set up nearby, suggesting he intended to spend the day working on his art.

When Pisch failed to return home, his family reported him missing. The National Park Service (NPS) initiated a search on October 10, 2020. Park rangers and volunteers scoured the area around Colonial Creek Campground and Diablo Lake. The initial search efforts included ground teams, canine units, and aerial reconnaissance, but there were no signs of Pisch.

Several campers and hikers reported seeing Pisch on the day of his disappearance. One eyewitness, a fellow camper, mentioned seeing him painting near the lake in the early afternoon. Another hiker reported seeing a man matching Pisch's description walking along a trail near the campground later in the day. However, these sightings did not provide any clues to his whereabouts after the evening of October 8.

As days turned into weeks, the search for Pisch intensified. The NPS, along with local law enforcement and search and rescue teams, expanded their efforts. They covered a larger area, including more remote and rugged terrains around Diablo Lake and Colonial Creek. Despite the extensive search, no additional evidence was found to indicate what might have happened to Pisch.

Several theories emerged regarding Pisch's disappearance:

- Accidental Fall: Given the rugged and often treacherous terrain of North Cascades National Park, one theory is that Pisch may have accidentally fallen into a ravine or off a cliff while exploring or looking for a perfect painting spot.
- Animal Attack: The park is home to various wildlife, including bears and mountain lions. Some speculate that Pisch could have encountered a dangerous animal and suffered an attack, though no evidence such as torn clothing or blood was found.
- Foul Play: Although there were no immediate signs of foul play, some consider the possibility

that Pisch might have encountered someone with ill intentions. However, this theory lacks supporting evidence, as there were no reports of suspicious individuals or activities in the area.

- Voluntary Disappearance: Another theory, albeit less likely according to those who knew him, is that Pisch chose to disappear voluntarily. His family and friends, however, dismissed this idea, citing his passion for painting and his close ties to his family.

As of the latest updates, the case remains unsolved. The NPS continues to keep the investigation open, and they periodically receive and follow up on new tips and leads. Pisch's disappearance has been featured in various media outlets, keeping public interest alive and encouraging anyone with information to come forward.

The disappearance of Alexander Pisch has had a profound impact on his family and the art community. His family has been actively involved in the search efforts, organizing volunteer groups and maintaining contact with law enforcement. They have also utilized social media to raise awareness about his case, hoping to reach someone who might have seen something relevant.

———

The mysterious disappearance of Alexander Pisch remains one of the many unsolved cases that haunt the scenic landscapes of North Cascades National Park. Pisch's family continues to seek closure, holding onto the hope that someday, they will find out what happened to their beloved artist.

# TWENTY-SIX

## STEPHEN "OTTER" OLSHANSKY

STEPHEN "OTTER" Olshansky, an experienced long-distance hiker, disappeared in late 2015 while trekking the Continental Divide Trail (CDT).

———

Stephen Olshansky, known affectionately as "Otter" within the hiking community, was no stranger to the challenges of long-distance hiking. He had completed the "Triple Crown" of hiking, which includes the Appalachian Trail, the Pacific Crest Trail, and the CDT. His love for the outdoors and his reputation as a resilient and knowledgeable hiker made his disappearance all the more shocking to those who knew him.

In early November 2015, Olshansky embarked on what would be his fifth thru-hike of the CDT. He began his journey in Chama, New Mexico, heading south. His plan was to hike through the winter, a risky endeavor given the harsh conditions and the likelihood of snowstorms.

Olshansky was last seen on November 14, 2015, when he was dropped off at Cumbres Pass, Colorado. He intended to hike back into New Mexico and continue his journey southward. His family and friends expected regular check-ins, but they heard nothing from him after he set off.

When Olshansky failed to check in, his family grew concerned and reported him missing. The search for Olshansky was challenging due to the vast and rugged terrain of the CDT. New Mexico State Police, along with the Continental Divide Trail Coalition (CDTC) and local search and rescue teams, launched a comprehensive search effort.

Search teams conducted aerial surveys and ground searches, covering extensive areas where Olshansky was thought to have traveled. Despite these efforts, no immediate clues were found. The search was complicated by reports of sightings of a man matching Olshansky's description in various locations throughout New Mexico and Arizona, leading investigators to chase numerous leads.

Several eyewitnesses claimed to have seen Olshansky after his disappearance. These sightings included:

- Near Quemado, NM: A man resembling Olshansky was reported walking along a road.
- Lordsburg, NM: A restaurant worker recalled seeing a man in a San Francisco 49ers pullover, which Olshansky was known to wear.
- Cuba, NM: A convenience store worker remembered speaking to a man who fit Olshansky's description.

Despite these reports, none of the sightings were confirmed, and the search teams were unable to locate Olshansky.

On January 4, 2016, Olshansky's body was discovered

by a group of hikers at the Lagunitas Campground, located off Forest Service Road 87 near Chama. He was found inside a Forest Service latrine, having sought shelter from the severe winter conditions. A note was found on the door, indicating that Olshansky knew he would not survive and had accepted his fate.

Olshansky's journals, recovered with his body, provided a haunting glimpse into his final days. According to these entries, Olshansky had attempted to survive despite the dire conditions. He documented his efforts to signal for help by burning a building, hoping the smoke would attract attention. Unfortunately, his signals went unnoticed.

The journals also revealed two suicide attempts. Olshansky tried to end his life by blocking a vent and filling the latrine with carbon dioxide, and later by cutting his wrist. Both attempts failed, and he ultimately decided to continue fighting for survival. He survived on horse feed he had found and tried to keep himself hydrated, but he eventually succumbed to the elements.

Several factors contributed to Olshansky's tragic end:

- Severe Weather Conditions: The winter weather on the CDT is harsh and unpredictable. Heavy snowfall and freezing temperatures can make survival extremely difficult, even for experienced hikers.

- Isolation: The remote nature of the CDT means that help is often far away. Olshansky's decision to hike alone during the winter increased the risks significantly.
- Delayed Search Efforts: The initial delay in launching a thorough search and the broad area that needed to be covered made it challenging for rescue teams to find Olshansky in time.
- Psychological Factors: Olshansky's journals indicated that he struggled with despair and hopelessness during his final days. His mental state likely deteriorated as his physical condition worsened.

Olshansky's death had a profound impact on the hiking community. He was well-known and respected among long-distance hikers, and his passing served as a stark reminder of the dangers inherent in their passion. The CDTC and other hiking organizations emphasized the importance of preparation, safety, and communication when undertaking such arduous journeys.

The tragedy of Stephen Olshansky's disappearance and death underscores several key lessons for hikers and rescuers alike:

- Preparation: Even the most experienced hikers must prepare thoroughly for extreme conditions, especially when hiking during winter months.

- Communication: Regular check-ins and having a reliable means of communication can make a significant difference in emergency situations.
- Emergency Planning: Hikers should have a detailed emergency plan, including knowledge of shelter locations and survival strategies for severe weather.
- Timely Search Efforts: Rapid response and focused search efforts are crucial in increasing the chances of a successful rescue.

―――――

The disappearance and death of Stephen "Otter" Olshansky remain a poignant chapter in the history of the Continental Divide Trail. His story serves as both a tribute to his adventurous spirit and a cautionary tale for those who follow in his footsteps. While his loss is deeply felt by his family, friends, and the hiking community, the lessons learned from his experience continue to shape the practices and safety measures of long-distance hiking today.

# TWENTY-SEVEN
## HEATHER LEANN CAMERON

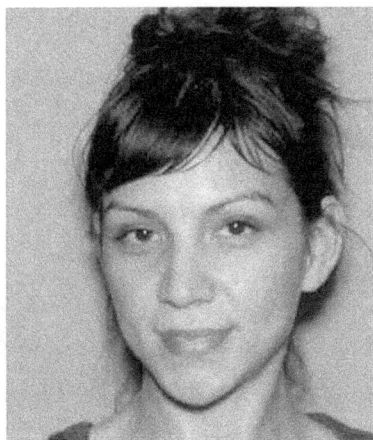

THE DISAPPEARANCE of Heather Leann Cameron is a haunting case that has puzzled investigators and distressed her loved ones since 2012. Heather, a 28-year-old mother of four, vanished under suspicious circumstances near the Keswick Dam in Shasta County, California.

————

Heather Leann Cameron was born on August 11, 1984. She was a member of the Grand Ronde Indian Tribe and spent much of her life in rural Redding, California. Heather had a tumultuous upbringing marked by her parents' struggles with drugs and alcohol. Despite these challenges, she shared fond memories with her cousin, Shannon Hauberg, of exploring the outdoors and enjoying nature during their childhood summers.

Heather had several tattoos, including tribal flowers on her back, a girl and a gun with tribal flowers on her left calf, and an unfinished character on her right thigh. These distinctive marks would later be crucial for identification purposes.

On August 18, 2012, Heather left a drug rehabilitation program and was picked up by her ex-boyfriend, Daniel Lusby. That afternoon, starting at 2:50 PM, Heather made three distressing 911 calls from the vicinity of the Keswick Dam Off-Highway Vehicle (OHV) Park. She used Lusby's phone to report that she had been drugged with heroin and needed urgent assistance. During these calls, a male voice could be heard in the background, adding to the ominous nature of the situation.

Despite the urgent nature of her calls, Heather was

never seen or heard from again after that day. Her estranged husband reported her missing two weeks later, prompting authorities to launch an extensive search of the remote area, which is characterized by steep hills, canyons, and poor phone reception. Unfortunately, these efforts turned up no trace of Heather.

The Shasta County Sheriff's Department led the investigation into Heather's disappearance. They conducted multiple searches using ATVs and on foot, scouring the rugged terrain around the Keswick Dam. Family members also participated in the search efforts, desperately hoping to find any clue that could lead to Heather's whereabouts.

Daniel Lusby, who was with Heather on the day she disappeared, was interviewed by police multiple times. Lusby claimed that he and Heather had gotten separated and that she had his phone when they parted ways. Despite being considered a person of interest, Lusby has never been charged in connection with her disappearance, and his phone was never recovered.

Heather's disappearance was classified as "endangered missing," given her history of substance abuse and the suspicious circumstances surrounding her case. She was known to regularly visit her children and maintain contact with their fathers, making her sudden and prolonged absence even more concerning.

The case of Heather Cameron has prompted numerous theories, each as troubling as the next. One prevalent theory is that Heather was a victim of foul play, possibly at the hands of someone she knew. The presence of a male voice during her 911 calls and the fact that she reported being drugged support this theory.

Another theory suggests that Heather may have succumbed to the harsh conditions of the area where she disappeared. The terrain around Keswick Dam is difficult to navigate, and the poor phone reception could have hindered her ability to seek help effectively. However, extensive searches by authorities and family members yielded no evidence to support this scenario.

Some speculate that Heather's disappearance might be linked to broader issues of violence against Native American women. National statistics highlight the alarming rates of violence, including homicide, that Native American women face. Heather's case fits into this disturbing pattern, raising questions about the systemic issues that may have contributed to her disappearance.

In the years following Heather's disappearance, her family has remained steadfast in their search for answers. Shannon Hauberg created a Facebook page, "Find Heather Cameron-Haller," to raise awareness and gather information that could lead to solving the case. A $5,000 reward has been offered for any information that leads to Heather's whereabouts or the resolution of her case.

The lack of closure has taken a significant toll on

Heather's family. They remember her as a loving mother who was always in contact with her children. The uncertainty surrounding her fate continues to haunt them, as they hold on to hope that one day they will find out what happened to Heather.

———

Heather Leann Cameron's disappearance is a tragic and unsettling mystery. Her case underscores the vulnerabilities faced by individuals with troubled backgrounds and highlights the broader issue of violence against Native American women.

If anyone has information regarding Heather Cameron's disappearance, they are urged to contact the Shasta County Sheriff's Department at (530) 245-6025 or the anonymous tip line at (530) 378-4491.

# TWENTY-EIGHT
## TODD HOFFLANDER

TODD HOFFLANDER, a 39-year-old experienced hiker and hunter, disappeared in late September 2010 during a hiking trip in the remote and rugged Windy Saddle area of Idaho County, Idaho.

———

Todd Hofflander was known for his outdoor skills and passion for hiking and hunting. On September 24, 2010, he embarked on a hunting trip with friends in the Hells Canyon Wilderness, a remote area known for its challenging terrain and breathtaking views. The group was well-prepared, equipped with the necessary gear for a multi-day trip in the backcountry.

On September 27, 2010, Todd and his companions decided to split up to cover more ground. Todd, whose knee was bothering him, opted to descend to the river while the others continued hunting. They planned to regroup later that day. When Todd failed to show up at the rendezvous point, his friends initially assumed he might have taken a different route or was delayed.

As hours turned into days, concern grew. The group retraced their steps and searched the area extensively but found no sign of Todd. On September 28, they reported him missing to the Idaho County Sheriff's Office, prompting an official search and rescue operation.

The search for Todd Hofflander was extensive and involved multiple agencies, including the Idaho County Sheriff's Office, local volunteers, and specialized search and rescue teams. Helicopters and drones were deployed to cover the vast and rugged terrain, and search dogs were brought in to track any scent trails. Despite these efforts, the search was hindered by the challenging conditions of the Hells Canyon Wilderness, characterized by steep cliffs, dense forests, and unpredictable weather.

Over the following weeks, search teams combed the area, focusing on likely paths Todd might have taken. The operation included ground searches, aerial surveys, and even underwater searches in the nearby river. Unfortunately, no trace of Todd was found, and the search was eventually scaled back, leaving his family and friends in a state of agonizing uncertainty.

Todd's disappearance sparked various theories and speculations. Some believed he might have suffered an injury or medical emergency, preventing him from reaching safety. Given his knee pain, it's possible he could have fallen or become immobilized in the difficult terrain.

Another theory suggested Todd might have become disoriented and wandered off course. The Hells Canyon Wilderness is notorious for its challenging navigation, and even experienced hikers can lose their bearings. The possibility of an animal attack was also considered, although no evidence supported this.

There were also darker speculations involving foul play, though no evidence pointed to any criminal activity. Todd's friends and family were adamant that he had no enemies and no reason to disappear voluntarily.

The case remained cold until April 26, 2020, when a hunter discovered human remains in the Bernard Creek area, a remote section of the wilderness not far from where Todd had disappeared. The hunter found a portion of a human skull, camping equipment, and a digital camera. Recognizing the potential significance of the find, he contacted the Idaho County Sheriff's Office.

The sheriff's office, along with the Idaho County Coroner, organized a recovery operation. Eight personnel were transported by jet boat to the site and hiked a mile inland to retrieve the remains. Among the items recovered was a backpack containing gear identified by Todd's wife as belonging to her husband. The digital camera's SD card contained photos of Todd, providing further evidence that the remains were likely his.

In late January 2021, the Idaho County Coroner, with assistance from the FBI, confirmed through DNA analysis that the remains were indeed those of Todd Hofflander. This confirmation brought a mix of relief and sorrow to his family, who had spent nearly a decade seeking answers.

The discovery of Todd's remains provided some closure but also raised new questions. How did Todd end up so far from his intended route? The items found with his remains indicated he was prepared for the wilderness, yet something had gone tragically wrong.

Photos from the camera revealed Todd's journey and provided a timeline of his last days. However, the exact circumstances of his death remain unclear. Theories suggest he might have succumbed to his knee injury, became dehydrated, or faced another unforeseen challenge that prevented him from reaching safety.

Todd Hofflander's disappearance and the subsequent search efforts highlight the dangers and unpredictability of wilderness areas like Hells Canyon. His case underscores the importance of safety measures and preparedness for outdoor adventures, even for experienced individuals.

For Todd's family, the confirmation of his death brought a measure of closure, allowing them to mourn and honor his memory. His story continues to resonate with the community and serves as a reminder of the enduring human spirit and the relentless pursuit of answers in the face of uncertainty.

———

The disappearance and eventual discovery of Todd Hofflander remain a poignant chapter in the annals of missing persons cases. Despite the challenges and the passage of time, the efforts of search teams, the dedication of his family, and the unexpected discovery by a hunter brought some resolution to a decade-long mystery.

JOE KELLER, a 19-year-old from Cleveland, Tennessee, vanished under mysterious circumstances on July 23, 2015, while on a run in the Rio Grande National Forest in Colorado. His disappearance has baffled authorities and left his family in a state of anguish, sparking extensive searches and numerous theories about what might have happened to him.

———

Joe Keller was a well-rounded and athletic young man, known for his involvement in sports and his community. He was a swim team coach and a volunteer at the Salvation Army. In the summer of 2015, Joe and his friends Collin Gwaltney and Christian Fetzner embarked on a 15-day cross-country road trip. Their journey brought them to the Rainbow Trout Ranch in Antonito, Colorado, a picturesque location surrounded by the vast Rio Grande National Forest.

On the afternoon of July 23, 2015, Joe and Collin decided to go for a run, a routine activity for the athletic friends. They set off together but soon separated as they ran at different paces. Collin returned to their meeting spot at the ranch after completing his run, but Joe never showed up. Concern quickly turned to panic as the hours passed without any sign of Joe. His cell phone had been left in his vehicle, eliminating the possibility of tracking him through GPS.

The search for Joe Keller began immediately and involved a massive effort from local authorities, volunteers, and specialized search teams. Drones, helicopters, dogs, infrared equipment, and searchers on horseback and on foot combed the area extensively. Despite these efforts, no trace of Joe was found in the initial days following his disappearance.

Joe's parents, Neal and Zoe Keller, traveled to Colorado to aid in the search for their son. They offered a $50,000 reward for any information leading to Joe's whereabouts. The Keller family also set up a Facebook page, "Find Joe Keller," to coordinate search efforts and gather tips from the public. This online presence garnered significant support and helped keep Joe's case in the public eye.

The investigation into Joe Keller's disappearance uncovered several theories and unconfirmed sightings. Collin Gwaltney, Joe's friend who had been running with him, expressed concerns that Joe might have fallen victim to foul play. He speculated that Joe could have been kidnapped, given the lack of physical evidence suggesting an accident or natural mishap.

Local authorities considered various scenarios, including the possibility that Joe had gotten lost or injured in the dense forest. However, the extensive search efforts, which included advanced technology and thorough ground searches, failed to turn up any substantial clues. Some tips came from psychics, one of whom suggested that Joe might be in Sedona, Arizona, but these leads did not produce any results.

Almost a year after Joe's disappearance, on July 6, 2016, former NFL player John Rienstra discovered human remains at the bottom of a cliff in the Rio Grande

National Forest. The remains were later confirmed to be Joe Keller's. The coroner determined that Joe had died from a fractured skull, likely sustained in a fall from the cliff. It appeared that Joe had attempted to climb the cliff, possibly losing his footing and falling to his death. The exact location where Joe's body was found had been searched previously, but it is believed that the dense vegetation and rugged terrain might have concealed his remains during earlier searches.

Joe Keller's death brought a tragic end to a year of uncertainty and anguish for his family and friends. The discovery of his remains provided some closure but also raised questions about how he ended up at the base of the cliff. The rugged and remote area of the forest where Joe's body was found highlighted the challenges faced by search teams in such difficult terrain.

In the wake of Joe's disappearance, his family and the local community continued to honor his memory. The "Find Joe Keller" campaign served as a testament to the determination and solidarity of those who sought to bring Joe home. His case also drew attention to the broader issue of people going missing in national parks and public lands, where the combination of vast wilderness and limited resources can complicate search and rescue efforts.

Joe Keller's disappearance and the subsequent discovery of his remains underscore the unpredictable and often perilous nature of wilderness environments.

For the Keller family, the loss of Joe was a devastating blow, compounded by the uncertainty and long search. Their unwavering commitment to finding their son and the support they received from the community are a testament to the enduring human spirit in the face of tragedy.

The case also serves as a sobering reminder of the risks associated with outdoor activities in remote areas. Even experienced and physically fit individuals like Joe can find themselves in dangerous situations with fatal consequences. The lessons learned from Joe Keller's disappearance emphasize the importance of preparation, communication, and awareness when venturing into wilderness areas.

———

The investigation into Joe Keller's disappearance may have concluded, but the questions and reflections it raises about safety, search protocols, and the human capacity for resilience and hope continue to resonate. As we remember Joe Keller, we are reminded of the importance of vigilance, preparedness, and community support in preventing and responding to such tragedies in the future.

# CHAPTER
# THIRTY

JOHN DEVINE

JOHN DEVINE, a seasoned hiker aged 73, disappeared under mysterious circumstances in Olympic National Park, Washington, on September 6, 1997. His case is one of the many perplexing disappearances in the park, characterized by harsh terrain and unpredictable weather.

———

John Devine was known for his love of the outdoors and his extensive hiking experience. Living in Sequim, Washington, he had spent many years exploring the rugged beauty of the Pacific Northwest. On September 6, 1997, Devine set out to hike Mount Baldy in the Buckhorn Wilderness Area, a part of Olympic National Forest known for its steep and challenging trails.

Devine was well-prepared for day hikes but did not carry overnight gear, suggesting he intended to return to camp by the evening. He was last seen by fellow hikers near the summit of Mount Baldy. When he failed to return to his campsite, concern quickly mounted among his family and friends, leading to an extensive search operation.

The search for John Devine was one of the most extensive in the history of Olympic National Park. It involved dozens of park rangers, search and rescue teams, and volunteers. The search operation, however, faced significant challenges, including treacherous terrain and rapidly deteriorating weather conditions.

Tragedy struck during the search operation when a Bell 205A-1 rescue helicopter crashed at approximately the 5,000-foot level of Mount Baldy, killing three people and injuring five others. The crash occurred shortly after takeoff from the mountainside, and the victims included Kevin Johnston, the pilot; Rita McMahon, a search volunteer who trained dogs for rescue missions; and Taryn Hoover, a seasonal park employee. The crash underscored the dangerous conditions and further complicated the search efforts.

Despite the setbacks, search teams continued to comb the area around Mount Baldy. The terrain was described as extremely rugged, with thick brush and steep drainages making the search difficult. Searchers focused on areas where Devine was most likely to have traveled, but as days passed without any clues, hope began to dwindle.

Sergeant Don Kelly of the Clallam County Sheriff's Office, which coordinated the search with the National Park Service, noted the challenges: "If he was walking around up there, we would have found him by now. And if he had fallen down and hurt himself, he probably wouldn't be alive".

The search was officially suspended on September 13, 1997, after six days of intensive efforts. The decision was made due to the lack of new leads and the increasingly adverse weather conditions, which made further search operations dangerous and unlikely to succeed. Park spokeswoman Barb Maynes stated, "The case isn't closed until Mr. Devine is found, of course, but it was the consensus of the search team that with bad weather setting in and six days without even a clue as to where he might be, the chances for survival are really quite slim".

The disappearance of John Devine has led to numerous theories, reflecting the mystery and intrigue surrounding many such cases in wilderness areas. Here are some of the primary theories:

- Accidental Fall: Given the treacherous terrain of Mount Baldy, one of the most plausible theories is that Devine accidentally fell and was unable to call for help. The thick brush and steep drop-offs in the area could easily conceal a body, making it difficult for searchers to find any trace of him.

- Medical Emergency: At 73, Devine might have suffered a medical emergency such as a heart attack or stroke, incapacitating him and preventing him from seeking help. The remote location and challenging environment would have made it difficult for him to survive without immediate assistance.
- Wildlife Encounter: Although less likely, an encounter with wildlife could have contributed to his disappearance. The Olympic National Park is home to various wildlife, including bears and mountain lions, which could pose a threat to a lone hiker.
- Foul Play: Some have speculated about the possibility of foul play, although there is no evidence to support this theory. Devine was an experienced hiker, familiar with the risks, and there were no indications of any suspicious activity in the area at the time of his disappearance.
- Misadventure: The most accepted theory is that Devine simply met with misadventure in an unforgiving wilderness. The combination of rugged terrain, unpredictable weather, and his

advanced age likely contributed to his inability
to return to safety.

The disappearance of John Devine had a profound impact on his family and the community. His wife, supported by their local church, faced the harrowing uncertainty of his fate. Friends and fellow hikers in Sequim mourned the loss of a well-respected member of their community. The tragic helicopter crash that claimed the lives of three searchers added another layer of sorrow to the already heartbreaking situation.

The case remains open, with park personnel continuing to watch for any signs of Devine during routine patrols. Despite the passage of time, the mystery of his disappearance lingers, a poignant reminder of the dangers inherent in exploring remote wilderness areas.

Eyewitness accounts from the day of Devine's hike were limited. He was seen near the summit of Mount Baldy, but no one witnessed any incident that could explain his disappearance. Fellow hikers described him as in good spirits and well-prepared for a day hike. However, the lack of substantial eyewitness testimony has made it challenging to piece together the events leading up to his disappearance.

Local authorities and search and rescue volunteers shared their experiences during the search. Jason Berry, a Park Service volunteer, described the area as "steep and rugged...the bushes are super thick and it's tough to walk down the drainages". The challenging conditions high-lighted the difficulties faced by search teams and the potential hazards that might have befallen Devine.

The disappearance of John Devine is one of several unsolved cases in Olympic National Park. Over the years, the park has seen multiple disappearances, each adding to the park's enigmatic reputation. Despite extensive search efforts and advanced search and rescue techniques, many cases, like Devine's, remain unresolved.

In the years following his disappearance, there have been periodic efforts to renew the search, driven by advances in technology and the persistent hope of finding closure. Devine's case continues to be referenced in discussions about the risks of solo hiking, particularly for older individuals, and the importance of being well-prepared for any eventuality.

———

John Devine's disappearance remains a haunting mystery. His case continues to baffle authorities and serves as a somber reminder of the potential dangers that hikers face.

The Devine family's hope for closure endures, as does the respect and admiration of the hiking community for a man who loved the wilderness. The unanswered questions surrounding his disappearance contribute to the enduring mystery and intrigue of Olympic National Park, a place of stunning beauty and hidden dangers.

# THIRTY-ONE

THERESA LYNN "TRENNY" GIBSON

ON OCTOBER 8, 1976, sixteen-year-old Theresa Lynn "Trenny" Gibson disappeared during a school field trip to the Great Smoky Mountains National Park. This mysterious case has baffled investigators and her family for decades.

———

Trenny Gibson was a sophomore at Bearden High School in Knoxville, Tennessee. She was described as a responsible and cautious teenager, known for her love of nature and hiking. On the day of her disappearance, Trenny, along with approximately 40 classmates, set out on a field trip to Clingmans Dome, the highest point in the Great Smoky Mountains.

The field trip was part of a horticulture class, and the students were expected to hike to Andrews Bald, a scenic grassy bald near Clingmans Dome. The weather on that day was reported to be cool and overcast with intermittent rain and fog, which later played a significant role in complicating the search efforts.

The students were allowed to hike at their own pace, resulting in several small groups spread out along the trail. Trenny was seen walking with different groups at various points throughout the day. Around 3:00 PM, she was last observed near Clingmans Dome, on a trail with steep drop-offs and dense undergrowth.

Trenny was last seen by her classmates near the Appalachian Trail intersection. She had been walking ahead of the group and reportedly stopped to look at something off the trail. When her classmates reached the spot, Trenny was gone. Initially, they assumed she had continued hiking, but when she failed to return to the meeting point at the scheduled time, concern grew.

By 4:30 PM, the National Park Service was notified, and a search was initiated. The search teams included park rangers, volunteers, and later, scent-tracking dogs and helicopters. The dogs picked up Trenny's scent along the Appalachian Trail, past the Clingmans Dome observation tower, and down to a roadside about 1.6 miles away. This led to speculation that she might have been picked up by a passing vehicle.

The search for Trenny was extensive, spanning several weeks and involving hundreds of volunteers. The efforts were hampered by poor weather conditions, including rain and fog, which limited visibility and made the terrain even more challenging. Despite the use of helicopters, ground searches, and tracking dogs, no trace of Trenny was found.

The scent-tracking dogs followed her trail to the base of the Clingmans Dome observation tower and along the roadside at Collins Gap, but the trail went cold from there. Items found in the area included cigarette butts and a partially filled can of beer, raising further questions about what might have happened to her.

Several students reported seeing Trenny at various points on the trail, but none could provide details about her final moments before she vanished. One of her classmates, Robert Simpson, had been walking with her shortly before she disappeared. He later became a person of interest due to some suspicious circumstances, including the discovery of Trenny's comb in his car and his conflicting statements. However, no concrete evidence

The investigation into Trenny's disappearance involved numerous law enforcement agencies, including the Tennessee Bureau of Investigation and the FBI. Despite extensive efforts, the case remains unsolved, leading to several theories about what might have happened to Trenny.

- Abduction Theory: The most prominent theory is that Trenny was abducted. The fact that the scent-tracking dogs followed her trail to the roadside suggests that she may have been picked up by a vehicle. Some believe that someone with ill intentions could have been waiting for an opportunity to take her, possibly following her from the observation tower.
- Voluntary Disappearance: Another theory is that Trenny may have voluntarily disappeared. This theory is supported by the statements of her classmate, Kim Pouncey, who suggested that Trenny might have wanted to leave and that someone was waiting for her in the park. However, this theory is less credible given that

Trenny left behind all her personal belongings, including money and identification.

- Accidental Fall or Getting Lost: The terrain where Trenny was last seen is known for its steep drop-offs and dense undergrowth. It is possible that she may have wandered off the trail, fallen, and become injured or lost. However, the extensive search efforts, including aerial searches and tracking dogs, did not find any evidence to support this theory.

- Foul Play by Someone Known: Suspicion fell on her classmate Robert Simpson due to the discovery of Trenny's comb in his car and his suspicious statements. Additionally, there was an incident involving a student named Kelvin Bowman, who had previously threatened Trenny. Bowman had broken into the Gibson residence in 1975 and was shot in the foot by Trenny's mother. Despite his threats, there was no evidence linking him to her disappearance, and he was reportedly attending classes the day she disappeared.

- Involvement of Park Visitors: Given the location and the presence of other visitors, it is possible that someone not associated with the school group could have encountered Trenny. The presence of cigarette butts and a beer can near where the scent trail ended suggests that someone might have been there.

Trenny's family has never given up hope of finding her. They have continuously worked with law enforcement, participated in media interviews, and kept her case in the public eye. They believe that Trenny was abducted and have expressed frustration over the lack of concrete evidence and leads.

In recent years, age-progressed images of Trenny have been released to aid in the search. These images depict what she might look like as an adult, offering a glimmer of hope that she could still be alive.

———

The disappearance of Theresa Lynn "Trenny" Gibson remains one of the most perplexing and heartbreaking cases in the history of the Great Smoky Mountains National Park. Her case highlights the challenges and limitations of search and rescue operations in rugged wilderness areas and underscores the enduring pain and uncertainty faced by the families of missing persons.

The case remains open, and anyone with information is urged to come forward to help bring resolution to this enduring mystery.

# THIRTY-TWO

STACY ANN ARRAS

THE DISAPPEARANCE of 14-year-old Stacy Ann Arras in 1981 remains one of the most haunting and perplexing mysteries in Yosemite National Park's history.

———

Stacy Ann Arras was a bright and adventurous teenager from Saratoga, California. On July 17, 1981, she joined her father and six others on a horseback trip to Yosemite National Park. The group planned a weekend excursion, intending to enjoy the park's breathtaking landscapes and natural beauty.

The group arrived at the Sunrise High Sierra Camp, an idyllic location offering stunning views of the surrounding wilderness. After unpacking, Stacy decided to take a short hike to a nearby lake, hoping to take some photographs. She invited her father to join her, but he declined, choosing instead to rest.

Stacy then asked one of the older members of the group, an elderly man, to accompany her. He agreed, and the two set off towards the lake. According to his account, Stacy quickly outpaced him and continued walking alone. She was last seen near the lake, approximately 100 yards from the camp.

When Stacy failed to return after a reasonable amount of time, the group became concerned and began searching the immediate area. They called out her name, scoured the trails, and checked the lake's perimeter, but there was no sign of her. As night fell, the searchers returned to the camp and reported Stacy's disappearance to the park rangers.

The following morning, a full-scale search operation

was launched. Yosemite's search and rescue teams, along with volunteers and other park personnel, combed the area. Helicopters, bloodhounds, and ground searchers covered a wide radius around the Sunrise High Sierra Camp. Divers searched the lake, fearing Stacy might have drowned, but found nothing.

The search effort was one of the largest in Yosemite's history, spanning several weeks. Despite the extensive and thorough search, no trace of Stacy—no clothing, camera, or personal items—was ever found. The searchers were baffled by the lack of evidence and the complete disappearance of a person in such a short distance from the camp.

The elderly man who had accompanied Stacy was the last person to see her. He described her as being in good spirits and eager to take photographs. He mentioned that she had walked ahead and disappeared from his sight around a bend in the trail. His account was corroborated by other members of the group who saw Stacy heading towards the lake.

Several hikers in the area were questioned, but none reported seeing Stacy. The lack of witnesses beyond the initial sighting by the elderly man added to the mystery.

Over the years, several theories have emerged regarding Stacy's disappearance. These theories range from plausible to highly speculative, reflecting the desperation to explain such a baffling case.

- Accidental Death: One of the most plausible theories is that Stacy might have slipped and fallen into a crevice or hidden ravine. Yosemite's rugged terrain is full of hazards, and a fall could have resulted in Stacy being concealed from searchers. However, the extensive search efforts, which included thorough examinations of potential hiding spots, make this theory less likely.

- Animal Attack: Another theory is that Stacy could have been attacked by a wild animal. Yosemite is home to black bears, mountain lions, and other wildlife. An animal attack could explain the suddenness of her disappearance. However, searchers found no signs of a struggle or animal tracks in the area.

- Abduction: Although less likely given the remote location, some speculate that Stacy might have been abducted. This theory raises questions about the presence of other individuals in the area and why no one saw or heard anything suspicious. The lack of evidence supporting this theory has made it one of the more controversial suggestions.

- Voluntary Disappearance: Some have speculated that Stacy might have chosen to disappear voluntarily. This theory is inconsistent with her behavior and the fact that she was in an unfamiliar wilderness area. Additionally, her close relationship with her family makes this theory highly unlikely.

- Supernatural or Paranormal Theories: As with many unsolved cases, there are those who propose supernatural explanations. Some suggest that Stacy might have encountered a portal or experienced some form of abduction by otherworldly beings. While these theories capture the imagination, they lack any tangible evidence and are not taken seriously by investigators.

Despite the passage of time, Stacy Ann Arras's disappearance remains an open case. Yosemite National Park and the National Park Service continue to receive tips and leads, though none have resulted in conclusive evidence. The case is periodically reviewed, and any new information is pursued diligently.

In recent years, advancements in technology, such as improved forensic techniques and the use of drones in search operations, have renewed hope that some clue might eventually be discovered. However, the vast and rugged terrain of Yosemite presents significant challenges.

Stacy's disappearance had a profound impact on her family. Her parents, George and Betty Arras, were devastated by the loss of their daughter. They actively participated in the search efforts and remained hopeful for many years. The uncertainty and lack of closure have been particularly difficult for the family to bear.

The Arras family's experience underscores the emotional toll that such disappearances take on loved ones. The hope for a miracle, combined with the harsh reality of the unknown, creates a persistent state of grief and unresolved questions.

Stacy Ann Arras's case has received significant media attention over the years, particularly within communities focused on missing persons and national park safety. Her disappearance is often cited in discussions about the importance of safety measures and preparedness when exploring wilderness areas.

The case has also highlighted the challenges faced by search and rescue operations in national parks. It serves as a reminder of the unpredictable nature of the wilderness and the need for constant vigilance and caution.

———

The Stacy Ann Arras case continues to baffle investigators and haunts those who were involved in the search.

# THIRTY-THREE
JOSEPH "JOE" WOOD

JOE WOOD WAS a 34-year-old African American writer and editor who had made significant contributions to literature and journalism. He was known for his work at the Village Voice and as an editor at The New Press. Wood was attending the Unity '99 journalism conference in Seattle when he decided to take a day trip to Mount Rainier National Park, an excursion that would mark his last known whereabouts.

On the morning of July 8, Joe Wood left his hotel in Seattle, rented a car, and drove nearly 90 miles to Mount Rainier National Park. He entered the park through the Nisqually entrance, planning a day of hiking and bird-watching. Joe was an experienced hiker and a passionate birder, often finding solace in the natural world despite the challenges he faced as a Black man in America.

He had informed friends that he planned to hike the Rampart Ridge Trail, a popular and relatively safe trail in the park. Joe was last seen around 10:00 AM by a park ranger who gave him directions. This was the last confirmed sighting of Joe Wood.

When Joe failed to return to his hotel and missed his flight back to New York, his family and friends grew concerned. They reported him missing, and a search operation was launched by the National Park Service. The initial search involved ground teams, helicopters, and sniffer dogs combing the Rampart Ridge area and surrounding trails. Despite extensive efforts, no trace of Joe was found.

The search was complicated by the vast and rugged terrain of Mount Rainier. Weather conditions varied, with fog and rain hampering visibility and search efforts. After several days, the official search was scaled back, although volunteers and private investigators continued to look for Joe for months afterward.

Several unconfirmed sightings of Joe were reported in the days following his disappearance. Some hikers claimed to have seen a man matching his description on less-traveled paths, but these sightings could not be verified. A significant clue emerged when Joe's rental car was found parked at the trailhead, containing his personal belongings, including his binoculars and bird-watching guide.

Despite the presence of these items, there were no signs of a struggle or foul play in the vehicle. Investigators found it puzzling that an experienced hiker like Joe would leave the trail without notifying anyone, especially given his cautious nature and familiarity with outdoor safety protocols.

Several theories have been proposed to explain Joe Wood's disappearance, each with varying degrees of plausibility:

- Accidental Fall or Injury: One of the most straightforward theories is that Joe might have fallen or suffered an injury while hiking. The rugged terrain of Mount Rainier, with its steep cliffs and hidden crevices, presents numerous hazards. A misstep could lead to a fatal fall, with the dense vegetation concealing the body from searchers.

- Animal Attack: Another theory suggests that Joe could have been attacked by a wild animal, such as a bear or mountain lion. While attacks on humans are rare, they are not unheard of. This theory is supported by the fact that no remains or personal items were found, as a large predator could potentially move or scatter them.
- Voluntary Disappearance: Some speculate that Joe might have chosen to disappear voluntarily. This theory, however, seems unlikely given Joe's professional commitments and close relationship with his family. He had recently been diagnosed with a heart condition, which could have influenced his decision-making, but there is no evidence to suggest he wanted to vanish.
- Foul Play: Given Joe's prominence and the fact that he was a Black man in a predominantly white area, some have theorized that he might have been the victim of a racially motivated crime. While this theory is difficult to prove without evidence, it remains a possibility in the minds of those who knew him well.

Joe Wood's disappearance had a profound impact on the literary and journalism communities. As a prominent figure, his absence was felt deeply by colleagues and friends. Memorial services were held, and numerous articles were written about his life and contributions. His disappearance also sparked discussions about the safety of people of color in outdoor spaces, highlighting the unique challenges they face in environments that can be hostile or unwelcoming.

Despite the passage of years, Joe Wood's case remains open. His family continues to hope for closure, and the National Park Service maintains an open file on his disappearance. Advances in technology, such as the use of drones and improved search techniques, offer some hope that new clues might one day emerge.

In the meantime, Joe Wood's legacy lives on through his writings and the memories of those who knew him. His disappearance serves as a stark reminder of the unpredictable nature of the wilderness and the enduring mysteries it holds.

———

The disappearance of Joseph "Joe" Wood is a haunting and unresolved chapter in the annals of missing persons cases. As with many such cases, the lack of closure leaves a lingering sense of unease and the hope that one day, answers might finally come to light.

# CHAPTER
# THIRTY-FOUR
## PAUL FUGATE

PAUL BRAXTON FUGATE, a seasoned park ranger, vanished without a trace on January 13, 1980, while on duty at Chiricahua National Monument in southeastern Arizona. His disappearance has remained one of the most enduring mysteries within the National Park

Service, with numerous theories but no definitive answers.

———

Paul Fugate was born on September 2, 1938, making him 41 years old at the time of his disappearance. He had worked at the Chiricahua National Monument for several years and was known for his deep knowledge of the park's flora and fauna. Fugate was an experienced outdoorsman and botanist, dedicated to his role as a park ranger. His long hair and beard set him apart from the typically clean-cut image of park rangers, reflecting his non-conformist attitude.

January 13, 1980, was a typical day at the Chiricahua National Monument. Fugate was the only permanent staff member on duty, assisted by a seasonal employee working as a clerk. Around 2:00 PM, Fugate left the visitor center, informing the clerk that he was going to check a nature trail and would return by 4:30 PM. He was last seen walking towards the park's entrance, dressed in his National Park Service uniform. He carried his keys but left his radio behind.

When Fugate did not return by the designated time, the clerk closed the visitor center and reported him missing. An extensive search was launched, covering the park's 12,000 acres of rugged terrain, which includes canyons, arroyos, and dense vegetation. Despite the thorough search efforts, no trace of Fugate was found. The initial search included park staff, local authorities, and volunteers, but the challenging landscape and lack of immediate clues hindered the efforts.

The investigation into Fugate's disappearance explored several theories, but none provided conclusive answers.

- Foul Play: One theory posited that Fugate might have stumbled upon illegal activities, such as drug smuggling or illegal immigration, which were prevalent in the area. Evidence supporting this theory included vehicle spinout tracks near a primitive road and indications of a struggle. Additionally, a park employee claimed to have seen Fugate in a pickup truck with two other men, looking "sad and dejected".
- Voluntary Disappearance: Some speculated that Fugate, known for his unconventional behavior and dissatisfaction with certain aspects of his job, might have chosen to disappear voluntarily. This theory was initially supported by the National Park Service's regional chief detective, who believed Fugate was "living with a paramour somewhere".
- Murder: In 1983, based on new leads, the Cochise County Sheriff's Office suggested that

Fugate had been murdered, and arrests were imminent. However, no charges were ever filed, and this theory remains unproven.

- Misadventure: Given the park's challenging terrain, some believed Fugate might have had an accident and succumbed to the elements. However, the absence of any physical evidence made this theory less likely.

The handling of Fugate's disappearance by the National Park Service (NPS) was fraught with controversy. In early 1981, the NPS formally terminated Fugate's employment, claiming he had abandoned his post. This decision led to financial hardship for his wife, Dody Fugate, who was asked to repay the salary she had received during the search period. It wasn't until 1986, after a re-examination of the case, that the NPS recognized the possibility that Fugate had not voluntarily disappeared, allowing Dody to claim survivor benefits.

Decades after Fugate's disappearance, new efforts to solve the case emerged. In 2018, the National Park Service increased the reward for information leading to Fugate's whereabouts from $20,000 to $60,000, indicating that new information had come to light. Despite these renewed efforts, the case remains unsolved, and Fugate's fate continues to be a subject of speculation and intrigue.

———

Paul Fugate's disappearance remains one of the most baffling mysteries in the history of the National Park Service. The lack of concrete evidence, combined with the various plausible theories, has left investigators and Fugate's family without closure.

# THIRTY-FIVE
## DENNIS MARTIN

ON JUNE 14, 1969, a seemingly routine family outing in the Great Smoky Mountains National Park turned into one of the most perplexing and enduring mysteries in American history. Dennis Martin, a six-year-old boy from Knoxville, Tennessee, vanished without a trace during a Father's Day weekend camping trip. This chapter explores the details of his disappearance, the extensive search efforts, eyewitness accounts, and the various theories that have emerged over the years.

The Martin family's annual tradition was to spend Father's Day weekend camping and hiking in the Great Smoky Mountains. This year, six-year-old Dennis, his older brother Douglas, their father William, and their grandfather Clyde ventured into the lush, green expanses of the park. It was Dennis's first overnight camping trip, and he wore a bright red shirt that made him easily visible against the natural backdrop.

The group reached Spence Field, a popular spot on the Appalachian Trail, where they met another family. The children decided to play a game of hide and seek. Dennis, Douglas, and two other boys planned to sneak up and surprise the adults. While the other boys jumped out, laughing, Dennis was nowhere to be seen. His red shirt, which should have been visible even among the trees, had vanished.

Realizing that Dennis was missing, his family began a frantic search of the immediate area. William Martin, convinced his son was nearby, called out for him, but received no response. As minutes turned into hours, the gravity of the situation became apparent. Clyde Martin hiked nine miles to the nearest ranger station in Cades Cove to report Dennis's disappearance.

By the time night fell, a severe thunderstorm hit the area, dropping three inches of rain and making the search conditions extremely difficult. Trails were washed out, and any potential tracks or clues were likely obliterated by the deluge. Despite these challenges, park rangers and the Martin family continued to search through the night, their efforts hampered by the weather and darkness.

The search for Dennis Martin officially began at 5:00 AM on June 15, 1969. Initially comprising a small group of National Park Service personnel, the search party quickly grew as news spread. Volunteers poured in from across the region, including park rangers, Boy Scouts, college students, firefighters, police officers, and even 60 Green Berets who happened to be training nearby.

At its peak, the search effort involved 1,400 people and covered a 56-square-mile area, making it the largest search operation in the history of the Great Smoky Mountains National Park. Helicopters, planes, and K-9 units were deployed, and searchers scoured every trail, ravine, and stream. Despite these massive efforts, no trace of Dennis was found.

The massive influx of volunteers, while well-intentioned, proved to be a double-edged sword. The sheer number of people trampling through the search area likely destroyed vital clues. Experienced trackers noted that the ground was so disturbed that it became impossible to differentiate between footprints made by Dennis and those of the searchers. Additionally, the heavy rain not only erased tracks but also made it difficult for search dogs to pick up any scent.

Reports from the time describe how the severe weather continued to hinder search efforts. Flash floods made some roads impassable, and low visibility from fog and rain complicated aerial searches. The searchers faced treacherous conditions, and many feared the worst for Dennis.

As days turned into weeks, various theories about Dennis's disappearance began to emerge. One of the most intriguing came from Harold Key, a tourist who reported hearing a "sickening scream" and seeing a disheveled man running through the woods on the afternoon Dennis disappeared. Key's sighting was approximately seven miles from Spence Field, and he claimed the man was carrying something over his shoulder that might have been clothing. Despite the potential significance, the FBI and park rangers concluded that there was insufficient evidence to link this sighting to Dennis's disappearance.

Several theories have been proposed over the years:

- Lost and Exposure: The most straightforward theory is that Dennis simply got lost and succumbed to the elements. Given the severe weather conditions and the challenging terrain, it's plausible that he wandered off, became disoriented, and eventually perished from exposure. However, the extensive search effort failed to find any physical evidence to support this theory.

- Animal Attack: Another possibility is that Dennis was attacked by a wild animal, such as a bear or feral pig, and carried off. The Great Smoky Mountains are home to various wildlife that could potentially pose a threat to a small child. Yet, no remains or signs of an animal attack were ever discovered.

- Abduction: Dennis's father, William, believed his son might have been abducted. The sighting reported by Harold Key lends some credence to this theory, suggesting that a person might have taken Dennis out of the park. However, there were no confirmed sightings of Dennis outside the park, and no ransom demands or communications were ever received by the family.

- Unusual Theories: Some have speculated that Dennis might have fallen victim to more unusual or far-fetched scenarios, including being taken by feral humans living undetected in the park. These theories, while intriguing, lack substantial evidence and are largely considered speculative.

The search for Dennis Martin officially ended on June 29, 1969, after two weeks of intense efforts. By then, over

13,000 man-hours had been spent searching, and the cost had risen to $50,000 (equivalent to over $400,000 today). Despite these efforts, no trace of Dennis was ever found.

The impact of Dennis Martin's disappearance extended beyond his family. The case led to significant changes in search-and-rescue operations within national parks. The National Park Service reviewed and updated its policies, emphasizing the need for better coordination and training for search efforts. The case also highlighted the limitations of involving large numbers of untrained volunteers in such operations.

Dennis Martin's disappearance remains an enduring mystery. Over the years, the case has continued to captivate the public's imagination, spawning books, documentaries, and countless discussions on online forums. The FBI eventually released their case file on Dennis Martin, which provided new details but no definitive answers.

———

Despite the largest search effort in the history of the Great Smoky Mountains National Park, the fate of the young boy remains unknown. Theories abound, from the plausible to the fantastical, but none have been proven.

For the Martin family, the pain of not knowing what happened to Dennis endures.

DEREK JOSEPH LUEKING

THE DISAPPEARANCE of Derek Joseph Lueking is one of the most baffling cases in the history of the Great Smoky Mountains National Park. On March 17, 2012, the 24-year-old from Louisville, Tennessee, vanished without a trace, leaving behind a trail of cryptic clues and unanswered questions.

———

Derek Lueking was described as a responsible and kind individual with a deep love for the outdoors. He graduated from Johnson University and worked as an aide at Peninsula Behavioral Health Center. An avid fan of survivalist shows, particularly Bear Grylls' "Man vs. Wild," Derek was fascinated by wilderness survival skills.

In the days leading up to his disappearance, Derek's behavior began to change. He didn't show up for work on March 15, and his family and friends started to worry when they couldn't reach him. Derek's grandfather had passed away a year earlier, and the anniversary of his death was approaching, which added to the family's concern given the close bond they shared.

Derek was last seen checking out of the Microtel Inn and Suites in Cherokee, North Carolina, at 4:00 AM on March 17, 2012. Surveillance footage captured him leaving the hotel alone, carrying a small daypack. His white Ford Escape was later found parked at the Newfound Gap area in the Great Smoky Mountains National Park. Inside the vehicle, authorities found a note that read, "Don't try to follow me."

The contents of Derek's car provided more clues but also deepened the mystery. He had purchased over $1,000 worth of camping gear, including maps of the park, a sleeping bag, a tent, a Gerber ax, a knife sharpener, a headlamp, a Bear Grylls survival tool pack, and granola bars, among other items. However, many of these items, including the tent and sleeping bag, were left in the car. This suggested that Derek had not planned for an extended stay in the wilderness or that his intentions might have changed suddenly.

The discovery of Derek's car at Newfound Gap prompted an extensive search operation. Park rangers, search and rescue teams, volunteers, and even helicopters scoured the area, covering more than 50 miles of trails. Despite the intensive efforts, no trace of Derek was found.

Eyewitnesses reported seeing Derek on the morning of March 17, but these sightings could not be confirmed. The search was complicated by the rugged terrain of the Smokies, which includes dense forests, steep cliffs, and numerous hidden hazards. The fact that it was a clear day with many visitors in the park yet no one saw Derek was puzzling to the authorities.

Several theories have been proposed to explain Derek's disappearance:

- Intentional Disappearance: Given the note found in his car and his purchase of survival gear, some believe that Derek intended to disappear and live off the grid. His fascination with survivalist shows supports this theory. However, the lack of significant gear and his minimal supplies make it unlikely he planned to survive long-term in the wilderness.

- Suicide: Another theory is that Derek went into the park with the intention of ending his life. The anniversary of his grandfather's death could have been a triggering factor. Yet, the purchase of expensive camping equipment seems contradictory to someone planning suicide.

- Accidental Death: Derek may have ventured off-trail and gotten lost or injured. The Smokies are known for their difficult terrain, and it's possible he succumbed to the elements or an accident. However, extensive searches yielded no evidence of his presence in the park.

- Foul Play: While less likely, the possibility of foul play cannot be entirely ruled out. There were no signs of struggle or evidence suggesting an attack, but the mysterious circumstances leave room for speculation.

- Psychological Factors: Some suggest that Derek might have been experiencing a mental health crisis. His recent behavior changes, coupled with the stress of his grandfather's anniversary, could indicate he was not in a stable state of mind. This could explain erratic actions and poor decision-making regarding his survival gear.

Derek's family has been relentless in their search for answers. They created a Facebook page, "Help Find Derek Lueking," to spread awareness and gather information. They also distributed thousands of flyers and coordinated search parties. Despite their tireless efforts, the case remains unsolved.

Tim Lueking, Derek's father, has expressed his gratitude for the ongoing search efforts by the park rangers and volunteers. He emphasized the importance of staying positive and keeping the search alive. The family continues to hold out hope that Derek will be found, or that someone will come forward with information that could shed light on his whereabouts.

———

The disappearance of Derek Joseph Lueking is a tragic and unresolved mystery. His family and friends continue to seek closure and answers, holding onto hope that one day, the mystery of Derek's disappearance will be solved.

The Great Smoky Mountains, with their beauty and

danger, serve as a reminder of the thin line between adventure and peril. Derek's story is a poignant example of how quickly and inexplicably someone can vanish, leaving behind only questions and heartache for those who loved him.

# CHAPTER
# THIRTY-SEVEN
## RANDY MORGENSON

RANDY MORGENSON WAS an experienced
backcountry ranger who vanished under mysterious
circumstances in July 1996. His disappearance in the
Sequoia and Kings Canyon National Parks in California

led to one of the most extensive search and rescue operations in National Park Service history.

––––––––

Randy Morgenson, at 51, was a veteran ranger with 28
years of experience in the High Sierra. Known for his
deep knowledge of the wilderness and his dedication to
preserving the pristine environment, he was a respected
figure among his peers. Randy's station at Bench Lake,
situated above 10,000 feet, served as his summer base,
from which he patrolled an 80-square-mile area. His
responsibilities included reporting on wilderness conditions, assisting hikers, and conducting search and rescue
operations.

On July 21, 1996, Randy left a note at his Bench Lake
station, indicating he would be away for two to three
days. Notably, he left behind his revolver, a Smith &
Wesson .357 Magnum, which was unusual for such a
seasoned ranger venturing into the wilderness. His note
mistakenly dated June instead of July, raising questions
about his state of mind. Randy's absence was reported
when he failed to check in via radio, prompting concern
among his colleagues.

The search for Randy Morgenson was launched on
July 25, 1996, and quickly became one of the most extensive in the park's history. Approximately 100 rescue
personnel scoured the rugged terrain, covering the 80-

square-mile area of his patrol. The search involved helicopters, dog teams, and dozens of volunteers. Despite
these efforts, no immediate trace of Randy was found.

One of the significant challenges faced by the search
teams was the late July rain, which obscured potential
tracks and made it difficult to determine Randy's direction. Colleagues speculated that his radio might have
malfunctioned, forcing him to hike to another station for
a replacement. This theory lost credibility as days passed
without any sign of Randy.

Randy Morgenson's disappearance was shrouded in
mystery, leading to various theories about his fate. Some
colleagues and investigators suggested that he might
have chosen to leave the park deliberately. However, this
theory was undermined by the discovery of his car in its
usual parking spot and no activity on his bank accounts
or credit cards.

Another theory considered was foul play, as Randy
had reportedly received threats on two occasions.
However, investigations ruled out these individuals as
suspects due to their strong alibis. There were also
rumors about Randy's personal life that added
complexity to the case. His marriage to Judi Morgenson
was strained, partly due to an affair he had with a fellow
ranger. Judi had filed for divorce, and Randy had
expressed feelings of depression and suicidal thoughts to
close friends.

The discovery of a letter from Randy, postmarked

July 19, 1996, sent to Judi's home in Sedona, Arizona, further complicated the investigation. Since there was no postal service in the national park, the letter raised suspicions that Randy might have left the area before his disappearance was reported.

The search for Randy Morgenson was officially called off in early August 1996 after no trace of him was found. It wasn't until July 2001, five years later, that a California Conservation Corps trail worker discovered his remains near a creek in a gorge in the Window Peak drainage, one of the remotest areas of the park. The discovery included a tattered shirt with Randy's badge, a backpack, and a boot with a leg bone protruding from it.

The location of the remains suggested that Randy had likely fallen through a snow bridge, breaking his leg, and possibly dying from the injuries and subsequent hypothermia. His body had been concealed under the ice during the initial search efforts, which explained why it was not found earlier.

Randy Morgenson's death has been subject to various interpretations and speculations. One compelling theory proposed by Eric Blehm, author of "The Last Season," is that Randy may have staged his disappearance to appear as though he had died on the job. This theory posits that Randy did so to ensure his wife, Judi, would receive a $100,000 government benefit, which would not be awarded in the case of a suicide. Blehm suggests that Randy's actions, such as sending the letter and leaving his revolver behind, were part of a carefully planned act to mislead the search teams.

Despite these speculations, the exact circumstances of Randy's death remain unclear. The rough terrain, combined with the natural elements and the time that had elapsed, left little definitive evidence to conclude what precisely happened.

Randy Morgenson's disappearance and the subsequent discovery of his remains have left a lasting impact on the National Park Service and those who knew him. His dedication to wilderness preservation and his tragic end have been memorialized in various ways. A peak in the Sierra Nevada, unofficially named Mount Morgenson, stands as a testament to his life and work. The peak is located near Mount Whitney and is a fitting tribute to a man who spent his life in the high country he loved.

———

While many questions about his disappearance and death remain unanswered, Randy's legacy as a devoted steward of the wilderness remains. His life and mysterious end continue to captivate and inspire those who seek to understand the untamed beauty and peril of the high Sierra.

# THIRTY-EIGHT

## CARL LANDER

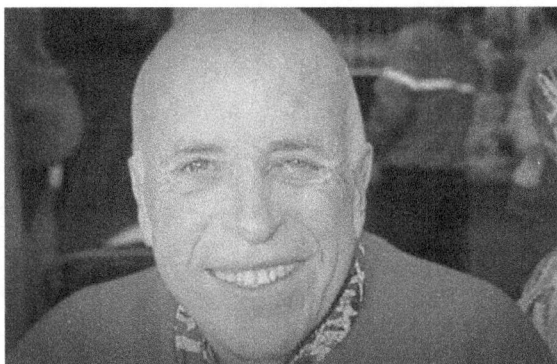

THE DISAPPEARANCE of Carl Herbert Landers is a perplexing case that has left investigators and his family searching for answers for over two decades.

———

Carl Herbert Landers was a 69-year-old man from Orinda, California, known for his passion for climbing and running. He was a member of the Orinda Road Runners, a local running club, and had an ambition to climb the highest peaks in every California county. At the time of his disappearance, he had already successfully climbed several peaks and was in excellent physical condition.

In May 1999, Carl planned a climb to the summit of Mount Shasta, a 14,162-foot volcanic peak in the Cascade Range, along with his friends Milton "Milt" Gaines, 64, and Barry Gilmore, 60, both of whom were also experienced climbers.

The trio set out on their journey to Mount Shasta on May 21, 1999. They left their motel at 4:00 AM, equipped with the necessary gear for the challenging ascent. The climb was arduous, with deep snow slowing their progress. They decided to camp overnight at the 50/50 Plateau, a known resting spot for climbers.

During the night, Carl began experiencing health problems, potentially exacerbated by his medication. Despite feeling unwell, he remained determined to continue the climb. Early on the morning of May 22, Carl decided to get a head start and left the camp around 9:00 AM, heading towards Lake Helen, a checkpoint before the final ascent to the summit.

Carl's friends, Milt and Barry, gave him a head start but expected to catch up with him shortly. When they reached Lake Helen and found no sign of Carl, they grew concerned. Milt followed Carl's trail, only to encounter a mysterious figure climbing swiftly. The climber was not Carl, and this sighting added to the confusion.

The friends immediately reported Carl missing. The Siskiyou County Sheriff's Department launched an intensive search operation, deploying a California National Guard air ambulance helicopter and a California Highway Patrol helicopter equipped with infrared sensing devices. Ground search efforts included U.S. Forest Service rangers, volunteers on skis, and search dogs. Despite the thorough search, no trace of Carl, his gear, or any clues to his whereabouts were found.

Several theories have emerged to explain Carl's mysterious disappearance, each as enigmatic as the last.

- Medical Emergency: One plausible theory is that Carl suffered a medical emergency, such as a heart attack or stroke, which led to his disappearance. Given his reported health issues and medication, this is a reasonable possibility. However, the lack of any physical evidence or remains complicates this theory.
- Accidental Fall: Another theory suggests that Carl may have accidentally fallen into a crevasse or a hidden part of the mountain, which would explain the absence of any visible traces. Mount Shasta's terrain is rugged

and treacherous, with many hidden dangers that could easily trap an unsuspecting climber.

- Foul Play: Although there is no direct evidence to suggest foul play, some have speculated that Carl's disappearance might involve other individuals. The sighting of the unidentified climber adds a layer of mystery, though there is no concrete evidence to support this theory.

- Animal Attack: Mount Shasta is home to various wildlife, including bears and mountain lions. An animal attack could explain the sudden disappearance, but again, the lack of any signs of struggle or remains makes this theory less likely.

- Supernatural and Unexplained Phenomena: Given Mount Shasta's reputation for supernatural folklore, some have speculated more outlandish theories involving extraterrestrial activity or other paranormal events. While intriguing, these theories lack empirical support and are not taken seriously by investigators.

The search for Carl Landers was one of the most extensive in Mount Shasta's history. Over several weeks, search and rescue teams scoured the mountain, covering the likely areas where Carl could have traveled. Helicopters conducted aerial searches, while ground teams combed through the snow and rocky terrain. Despite these efforts, not a single clue emerged.

The use of infrared technology aimed to detect any heat signatures that could indicate Carl's presence, but these efforts also came up empty. Search dogs were employed to pick up Carl's scent, but they too were unsuccessful. The lack of any evidence baffled searchers and added to the mystery of Carl's disappearance.

Carl Landers' disappearance had a profound impact on his friends, family, and the wider community. His family was left with an agonizing lack of closure, compounded by the fact that no remains or belongings were ever found. The uncertainty surrounding Carl's fate made it difficult for his loved ones to move on.

The case also highlighted the risks associated with mountain climbing, even for experienced climbers. It underscored the importance of preparedness, awareness of one's physical condition, and the potential dangers inherent in such activities.

The case of Carl Landers remains open and unsolved. The Siskiyou County Sheriff's Department continues to treat the disappearance as an active case, periodically reviewing any new information that might come to light. Despite the passage of time, Carl's story continues to intrigue and perplex those who hear it.

Carl's disappearance has been featured in various media outlets, including television shows, podcasts, and articles dedicated to unsolved mysteries. These efforts aim to keep the case in the public eye, hoping that new leads or information might eventually surface.

————

The disappearance of Carl Herbert Landers on Mount Shasta remains unresolved, leaving Carl's family and friends with unanswered questions and an unfulfilled quest for closure.

# THIRTY-NINE
## SAMUEL BOEHLKE

THE DISAPPEARANCE of Samuel Boehlke is one of the most puzzling cases of a missing person in a national park. On October 14, 2006, the eight-year-old boy vanished while hiking with his father, Ken Boehlke, at Crater Lake National Park in Oregon.

Samuel "Sammy" Savage Becker Boehlke was an active and curious child, known for his love of outdoor activities such as hiking and fishing. Born on August 10, 1998, in Portland, Oregon, Samuel was diagnosed with Asperger's Syndrome, a high-functioning form of autism. This condition made him particularly sensitive to bright lights and loud noises and sometimes caused him to react in ways that might seem unusual to others.

On the morning of October 14, 2006, Samuel and his father, Ken Boehlke, were staying at the Diamond Lake Resort, located about nine miles from Crater Lake National Park. The father-son duo decided to spend the day exploring the park, renowned for its breathtaking views and serene environment. They parked near the Cleetwood Cove Overlook and began their hike toward the lake.

At around 4:00 PM, while hiking near the Cleetwood Cove trail, Samuel suddenly ran ahead of his father, crossed the road, and disappeared into the woods. Ken, initially believing that Samuel was playing a game, followed him but soon lost sight of his son. Despite his efforts to catch up, Samuel had vanished by the time Ken reached the woods.

Ken Boehlke quickly reported his son missing, prompting park rangers and volunteers to initiate a search. The initial search effort included over 145 trained personnel, search dogs, and helicopters equipped with heat-sensing cameras. Despite these efforts, there was no sign of Samuel. The weather conditions at the time were cold and snowy, with subfreezing temperatures that would have made survival without shelter extremely difficult for an eight-year-old boy.

The search for Samuel Boehlke continued intensively for about a week, covering an area of approximately six square miles (4,000 acres). Search teams included experts from various counties and states, as well as specialist rescue teams from Mount Hood and Mount Rainier. Despite the involvement of these experienced searchers and the use of advanced technology, no trace of Samuel was found.

One search dog appeared to pick up Samuel's scent a few days after his disappearance, but other dogs could not confirm the scent trail. The area received between four to six inches of snow shortly after Samuel went missing, which both helped and hindered the search efforts by preserving tracks but potentially covering other crucial clues.

Numerous theories have emerged over the years regarding Samuel's disappearance. Here are some of the most prominent:

- Accidental Death: The most widely accepted theory is that Samuel became lost or injured in the dense woods and succumbed to the harsh weather conditions. Given his lack of wilderness survival training and the subfreezing temperatures, it is plausible that he could not have survived long without shelter.

- Animal Attack: Another theory suggests that Samuel may have encountered a wild animal. While attacks by large predators like bears or mountain lions are rare in Crater Lake National Park, they are not impossible. However, no evidence, such as blood or clothing remnants, has been found to support this theory.

- Abduction: Some have speculated that Samuel might have been abducted. However, investigators and Samuel's family have largely dismissed this theory due to the lack of evidence suggesting foul play. The area where Samuel disappeared is relatively remote, making it less likely for an abductor to be present without drawing attention.

- Voluntary Disappearance: Given Samuel's condition, it is possible that he might have been hiding, thinking it was a game, and moved further away from the search areas. His history of hiding and being difficult to find, as noted by the director of the Sellwood

Community Center where Samuel previously attended day camp, supports this theory. However, it is unlikely that an eight-year-old could survive for long under such circumstances without leaving any trace.

The official search for Samuel Boehlke was scaled back on October 23, 2006, after extensive efforts failed to locate him. Despite the cessation of the large-scale search, intermittent efforts continued, particularly when conditions allowed for better visibility and accessibility in the park. In November 2006, Samuel's family held a memorial service for him, acknowledging the slim chances of his survival but continuing to hope for answers.

In 2016, the documentary "Missing 411," which investigates mysterious disappearances in North American wilderness areas, featured Samuel's case. This brought renewed attention to his disappearance and highlighted the perplexing nature of cases like his.

———

The disappearance of Samuel Boehlke remains an unresolved and haunting mystery. The Boehlke family, along with the wider community, continues to hope for closure and answers about what happened to their beloved son and brother on that fateful day at Crater Lake.

As with many unsolved cases, the hope remains that one day, new evidence or breakthroughs in search techniques might finally provide the answers that Samuel's family and the community have been seeking for so long.

# CHAPTER
# FORTY

ANGELA MARIE FULLMER

ANGELA MARIE FULLMER'S disappearance is a perplexing and heart-wrenching mystery that has left her family and investigators searching for answers for over two decades. Angela, a 34-year-old mother of five, vanished on December 15, 2002, under circumstances that remain unclear and suspicious.

———

Angela Marie Fullmer, also known as Angie, was born on February 28, 1968. At the time of her disappearance, she was living in Mount Shasta, California. Angie was described as a devoted mother to her five daughters, ranging in age from seven to seventeen, and had another child she had placed for adoption. Known for her vibrant personality and love for her family, Angie's sudden disappearance was out of character and deeply troubling.

On December 15, 2002, Angie was last seen in the company of her boyfriend, Thomas O'Connell. According to O'Connell, they had spent the weekend drinking and decided to go for a drive to the Twin Pines area near Lake Siskiyou, west of Mount Shasta. They left around 2:45 p.m., but the outing soon took a distressing turn.

O'Connell reported that they had an argument over mud tracked into the pickup truck. Angie allegedly left the vehicle in frustration and walked into the forest towards South Fork Road near an old logging road. O'Connell claimed that while he was cleaning out his truck, he heard a car door slam and an engine start, assuming Angie had gotten a ride from someone else.

O'Connell reported Angie missing at approximately 2:45 a.m., about eight hours after she was last seen. The delay in reporting raised suspicions, but O'Connell was not initially considered a suspect. Authorities launched a search operation, focusing on the forested area where Angie was last seen. However, inclement weather and the dense terrain hampered search efforts, yielding no results.

The Siskiyou County Sheriff's Department led the investigation. They interviewed O'Connell and other potential witnesses, but no substantial leads emerged. Angie's family and friends were adamant that she would not have left voluntarily, especially without contacting her children or accessing her bank accounts.

Several eyewitness reports surfaced in the days and months following Angie's disappearance. Some residents claimed to have seen a woman matching Angie's description near the area where she was last seen, but these sightings could not be verified. Additionally, O'Connell's account of hearing a car door and engine raised the possibility that Angie had been picked up by someone, either voluntarily or under duress.

Angie's disappearance has given rise to numerous theories, each suggesting different scenarios of what might have happened to her.

- Abduction: One prevailing theory is that
  Angie was abducted, possibly by someone she

knew or a stranger. The reported sound of a car door and engine starting lends some credence to this theory. However, there has been no concrete evidence to support this.

- Foul Play by an Acquaintance: Given the argument between Angie and O'Connell and the delay in reporting her missing, some speculate that O'Connell may have been involved in foul play. However, he has consistently denied any involvement, and there has been no evidence to implicate him directly.

- Voluntary Disappearance: Some have suggested that Angie might have left voluntarily, perhaps to escape personal issues or responsibilities. However, this theory is widely dismissed by her family, who argue that she would never abandon her children and had made plans for Christmas, indicating she intended to return.

- Accidental Death: Another theory is that Angie may have suffered an accident in the forest and succumbed to the elements. Despite extensive searches, no trace of her has ever been found, making this theory less likely but still possible.

In August 2003, a man walking his dog found human

bone fragments in the Shasta-Trinity National Forest near the North Shore Road, close to where Angie was last seen. Initially, authorities believed these remains could be Angie's, but forensic analysis revealed they were cremains scattered during a memorial ceremony, unrelated to Angie's case.

Angie's family has never given up hope of finding her. They have conducted their own searches, distributed flyers, and appeared on television shows to keep her case in the public eye. The lack of closure has been agonizing, but they remain determined to uncover the truth.

As of the latest updates, Angie's case remains unsolved. The Siskiyou County Sheriff's Department continues to receive tips and follow up on leads, but no significant breakthroughs have been made. The case has been featured in various media outlets, including local news reports and missing persons databases, to generate new leads and keep the investigation active.

Angie's family and friends continue to advocate for her, holding vigils and commemorative events to honor her memory and remind the public of her unresolved case. They hope that advancements in technology, such as improved DNA analysis and digital forensics, may eventually provide new avenues for investigation.

———

The disappearance of Angela Marie Fullmer is a tragic mystery that has left a void in the lives of her loved ones and the Mount Shasta community. Despite the passage of time, the search for answers continues. Her family remains hopeful that one day they will uncover the truth and bring Angie home.

For anyone with information about Angie's disappearance, please contact the Siskiyou County Sheriff's Department at (530) 841-2911. Every piece of information, no matter how small, could be crucial in solving this case.

# CHAPTER
# FORTY-ONE
## MICHAEL BRYSON

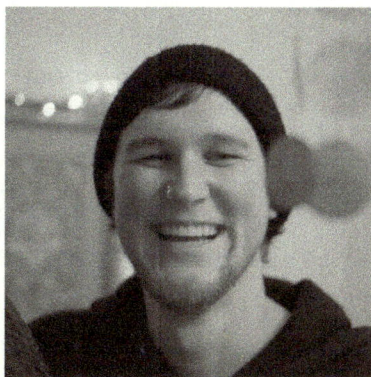

MICHAEL BRYSON'S disappearance remains one of the most perplexing and troubling cases in recent history. On a quiet evening in early June, Michael vanished without a trace, leaving behind a community in turmoil, a family in despair, and a plethora of unanswered questions.

———

Michael Bryson was reported missing by his family on June 5th, following a routine evening out with friends. According to his parents, Michael had attended a local concert at the Hillside Amphitheater in their small hometown. Friends and family described Michael as a responsible and reliable young man, making his sudden disappearance all the more alarming.

The first call to the police was made at 11:45 PM by Michael's mother, Linda Bryson, who expressed her growing concern after failing to reach her son on his cellphone. Officers were dispatched immediately, initiating what would become an exhaustive search operation.

Upon receiving the missing person report, the police began by interviewing friends and family who had seen Michael last. Officers obtained descriptions of Michael's appearance on the night he disappeared: he was wearing a black jacket, blue jeans, and a pair of white sneakers. His last known location was the parking lot of the concert venue, where he was seen speaking with an unidentified man around 10:30 PM.

Investigators quickly secured the area and began a thorough search, using both ground units and aerial support. A command post was established at the venue, and officers combed through nearby woods, fields, and water bodies. Sniffer dogs were also brought in to aid in the search.

The local community mobilized in support, distributing flyers, organizing volunteer search parties, and sharing information on social media platforms. Despite these efforts, no substantial leads emerged in the early days of the investigation.

Several eyewitnesses came forward with information that provided a fragmented picture of Michael's last known movements. Among the most credible accounts were those of his friends, who had been with him at the concert:

- Emma Watson, a close friend, reported that Michael seemed distracted and received multiple phone calls throughout the evening. She noted that he stepped away several times to take the calls but did not share details about who he was speaking with.
- John Miller, another friend, mentioned that Michael appeared to be in a hurry to leave just before the concert ended. He saw Michael walking towards the parking lot but did not see him interact with anyone suspicious.
- Sara Lewis, an attendee at the concert, told police she saw Michael talking to a man near a black SUV. She described the man as being in his late 30s, with short dark hair and wearing a leather jacket. This sighting became a focal point in the investigation as it

suggested that Michael may have met someone intentionally.

Further inquiries revealed that Michael had received a series of text messages from an unknown number shortly before his disappearance. The police traced the number to a disposable phone, complicating their efforts to identify the sender.

As the investigation progressed, several theories about Michael's disappearance began to surface. Each theory was meticulously examined by the police, though none could be conclusively proven.

- Abduction: The most prominent theory was that Michael had been abducted. The sighting of the man near the black SUV suggested the possibility of foul play. Investigators explored the idea that Michael might have been lured away by someone he knew or coerced by a stranger.
- Voluntary Disappearance: Another theory considered was that Michael had chosen to disappear voluntarily. This was based on the observation that he appeared distracted and anxious in the days leading up to his disappearance. Friends and family, however, vehemently denied this possibility, citing his close ties and future plans.

- Accidental Death: The possibility of an accident was also examined. The dense woods and nearby river posed significant hazards, and search teams were dispatched to thoroughly investigate these areas. However, no evidence was found to support this theory.

- Criminal Involvement: Some speculated that Michael might have been involved in something illicit, such as drug dealing or other criminal activities. This theory emerged due to the mysterious phone calls and the presence of the unidentified man. Nonetheless, Michael's background and lifestyle did not align with this notion, leading many to dismiss it as unlikely.

Forensic teams scoured Michael's car, which was found parked at the concert venue. The vehicle yielded little information, with no signs of struggle or any forensic evidence pointing to foul play. Michael's phone records were analyzed, but the disposable phone that contacted him proved to be a dead end.

The search of the surrounding areas, including the river and wooded areas, was extensive. Divers scoured the river, and search dogs were used in the woods, but no trace of Michael was found. This lack of physical evidence frustrated investigators and left many questions unanswered.

Michael's disappearance had a profound impact on the local community. Vigils were held, and a social media campaign was launched to keep Michael's story in the public eye. The Bryson family made numerous public appeals, pleading for any information that could lead to Michael's whereabouts.

Linda Bryson, Michael's mother, spoke at several press conferences, often breaking down as she described her son and the pain of not knowing what had happened to him. "Michael is a wonderful son, a caring brother, and a dear friend to many. We just want him home," she said tearfully during one such appeal.

The police also faced criticism from some community members who felt that the investigation was not progressing swiftly enough. In response, law enforcement officials reassured the public that every possible lead was being followed and that the case remained a top priority.

The media played a significant role in keeping Michael's disappearance in the public eye. News outlets covered the story extensively, with many drawing parallels to other high-profile missing person cases. This media attention brought in several tips from the public, though none led to a breakthrough.

The pressure from the media also kept the police accountable, ensuring that the investigation remained active and visible. However, this attention also had its downsides, with the Bryson family often feeling over-whelmed by the constant scrutiny.

As of the latest updates, Michael Bryson remains missing. The police continue to follow up on new leads and tips, but the case grows colder with each passing day. The Bryson family has hired a private investigator to conduct an independent inquiry, hoping that a fresh perspective might uncover new information.

The community remains supportive, with periodic searches and fundraisers to support the ongoing investigation. Michael's case has also prompted local authorities to review and improve their protocols for handling missing person reports, aiming to prevent similar occurrences in the future.

———

The disappearance of Michael Bryson is a haunting mystery that leaves a lingering question mark over the small town he called home.

# CHAPTER
# FORTY-TWO
## DERRICK ENGEBRETSON

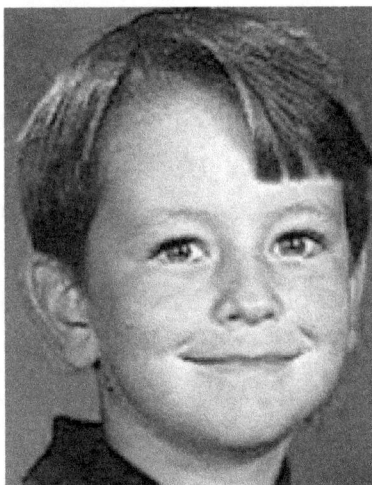

THE CRISP WINTER air was thick with excitement as eight-year-old Derrick Engebretson set out with his father, Robert, and grandfather, Bob, to find the perfect

Christmas tree in the Winema National Forest near Rocky Point, Oregon. Clad in a blue snowmobile suit, denim jacket, and camouflage-print boots, Derrick was eager to cut down a tree for the family. As the trio trekked through the snowy forest, the joy of the holiday season was palpable.

However, as the day wore on, the festive spirit turned to panic. Derrick, who had wandered away momentarily, was nowhere to be found. His father and grandfather's calls echoed through the dense forest, but there was no response. The winter storm that had started to blow in complicated matters further, covering the forest floor with several feet of snow and obliterating any trace of the young boy's path.

The alarm was raised quickly, and search efforts began almost immediately. Local law enforcement, volunteers, and search and rescue teams mobilized, using everything from sniffer dogs to helicopters to comb the area. Despite these extensive efforts, the heavy snowfall and harsh conditions severely hampered the search operations. For days, searchers found no sign of Derrick, and the hopes of finding him alive began to dwindle as the temperatures plummeted below zero.

Amidst the search, volunteers discovered a few items that sparked brief moments of hope. A candy wrapper and a Bonanza School bookmark were found near Rocky Point, raising the possibility that Derrick had been in the area. Additionally, a makeshift shelter made from fir boughs was discovered under some fallen logs. However, tracker dogs could not detect Derrick's scent at the site, and further searches yielded no significant clues.

As the search continued, a disturbing theory began to take shape. An eyewitness reported seeing an unidentified man struggling with a boy near the road on the day of Derrick's disappearance. Initially dismissed as possibly a misunderstanding, this sighting gained traction when another witness reported seeing a man in a black two-door Honda asking for directions in the forest on the same day.

Further complicating the case, some graffiti appeared on a bathroom wall near Burns, Oregon, in 1999, claiming that Derrick had been killed and buried. The FBI investigated but ultimately dismissed it as a cruel hoax. Similarly, a bone discovered in 2000, initially raising hopes, turned out to be from a deer.

In 2002, the investigation took a significant turn when Frank J. Milligan, a convicted child rapist and attempted murderer, became a prime suspect. Serving a sixty-year sentence for other heinous crimes, Milligan had confessed to abducting and killing Derrick. He provided details, claiming that Derrick had made it out of the woods and that he had picked him up by the road. Milligan even offered to lead investigators to Derrick's body in exchange for avoiding the death penalty. Despite this, searches based on Milligan's directions turned up nothing, and he later recanted his confession.

Milligan's history was chillingly similar to the circumstances of Derrick's disappearance. On July 11, 2000, Milligan had lured a ten-year-old boy in Dallas, Oregon, with an offer of money, then abducted, sexually assaulted, and attempted to murder him. The boy survived and identified Milligan, leading to his conviction. A fellow inmate's letter claiming Milligan had boasted about killing Derrick added weight to suspicions against him, but without concrete evidence, the case against him stalled.

Despite exhaustive searches and numerous tips, no definitive evidence has surfaced to explain what happened to Derrick. Theories about his fate remain varied and contentious. Some believe he succumbed to the harsh elements and his remains were scattered by wildlife. Others suspect abduction by Milligan or another predator. The discovery of animal bones and the cold temperatures that night support the theory of Derrick dying from exposure. Yet, the eyewitness accounts and Milligan's suspicious behavior keep the possibility of foul play alive.

Derrick's family has never stopped seeking answers. They continue to visit the forest, leaving balloons tied to trees each year on his birthday, hoping against hope that one day they will find closure. The case remains open, with law enforcement and the family holding onto the slimmest chances that Derrick might still be alive somewhere.

———

The disappearance of Derrick Engebretson is a tragic loss and the enduring uncertainty have left a permanent scar on all those involved, a reminder of the thin line between ordinary life and unthinkable tragedy.

# FORTY-THREE
ALISSA MARIE MCCRANN

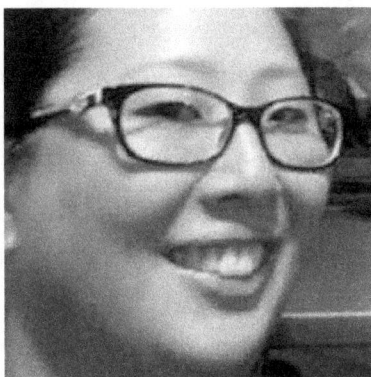

ON DECEMBER 19, 2015, Alissa Marie McCrann, a 37-year-old mother from Portland, Oregon, went missing near the scenic Multnomah Falls.

———

Alissa McCrann was an avid hiker and runner, often frequenting the trails around Multnomah Falls. On the day of her disappearance, she informed friends that she would be spending the day hiking in the area. She was well-known in her community as a dedicated mother and reliable friend, making her sudden disappearance all the more alarming.

On the morning of December 19, 2015, Alissa left her home in Portland and drove to Multnomah Falls, about 30 minutes away. She was last seen around 10 AM, based on a social media post she made from the trail. The weather that day was typical for Oregon in December—cool and damp, with potential for rain.

Alissa's vehicle, a silver SUV, was found parked in the Multnomah Falls parking lot on December 22, 2015. This discovery was made after her family reported her missing, having not heard from her since her last social media post. The vehicle was locked, and there were no immediate signs of foul play.

Upon discovering her vehicle, search and rescue teams were deployed to comb the area around Multnomah Falls. The initial search involved over 150 miles of trails, with teams utilizing dogs, drones, and thermal imaging cameras. Despite these efforts, no trace of Alissa was found.

Several hikers reported seeing a woman matching Alissa's description on the day she disappeared. One couple recalled seeing her near the top of the falls, while another group mentioned passing her on the trail. However, none of these sightings provided concrete leads, and her exact whereabouts remained unknown.

————

Evidence and Theories:

- Accidental Fall: One theory posits that Alissa may have slipped and fallen from one of the trails. The terrain around Multnomah Falls is rugged and steep, with numerous spots where a misstep could prove fatal. However, no evidence of such an incident was found despite extensive searches.
- Voluntary Disappearance: Another theory is that Alissa might have chosen to disappear voluntarily. This theory is less favored, given her strong ties to her family and community. Those who knew her best insist she would never abandon her responsibilities or her loved ones without any communication.
- Foul Play: The possibility of foul play cannot be ruled out. Although no immediate signs of struggle were found in her vehicle or on the trails, it is conceivable that someone could

have abducted her. This theory is supported by the fact that her phone and personal belongings were missing, possibly taken by someone involved in her disappearance.

- Exposure and Hypothermia: Given the weather conditions, it is also possible that Alissa succumbed to exposure and hypothermia. Unprepared hikers can easily get lost or injured, and the cold temperatures can be deadly without proper gear and shelter.

The search for Alissa McCrann continued sporadically for years after her disappearance. Volunteer search parties, organized by her family and friends, frequently scoured the area for any signs of her. The community held vigils and fundraisers to support the ongoing search efforts and to keep her story alive in the public consciousness.

Alissa's disappearance had a profound impact on her family. Her children struggled with the sudden loss of their mother, and her parents and siblings were left grappling with unanswered questions. The uncertainty of not knowing what happened to her was a constant source of pain and frustration.

———

The case of Alissa Marie McCrann remains one of the many unsolved disappearances in the United States. Despite the best efforts of law enforcement, search and rescue teams, and her loved ones, her fate remains unknown.

# FORTY-FOUR
BOB BOBO

ON THE QUIET evening of May 13, 2008, Bob Bobo vanished without a trace, leaving her small town bewildered and her family devastated. The investigation into her disappearance commenced promptly, with local authorities pouring over every available detail, yet the mystery only deepened with each passing day.

The last confirmed sighting of Bob Bobo was around 10:30 PM when she was seen leaving a local diner where she worked part-time. The security footage from the diner showed her walking towards her car, a beat-up sedan parked under a streetlamp in the adjacent lot. She appeared to be in a hurry, glancing over her shoulder multiple times before getting into her vehicle and driving off.

Approximately thirty minutes later, a resident living on the outskirts of town reported seeing a car matching the description of Bob's vehicle parked erratically by the side of Route 68, the road that leads out of town. The resident, an elderly woman named Mrs. Peterson, noticed the car because its hazard lights were flashing. She recalled seeing a tall man standing beside the vehicle, seemingly engaged in a heated conversation with someone inside the car.

At 11:45 PM, another report came in from a truck driver, Mike Reynolds, who was passing through Route 68. He noticed the same car abandoned by the roadside, its hazard lights still on, but this time there was no sign of the man or anyone else around. Reynolds, concerned about a potential accident, stopped to check but found the car empty and no one in the immediate vicinity. He called the local police to report the abandoned vehicle.

When the police arrived at the scene, they found Bob's car unlocked and her purse lying on the passenger seat, untouched. The car's keys were still in the ignition, and her phone was discovered on the ground a few feet away from the vehicle, its screen cracked but still functioning. There were no immediate signs of a struggle, but a closer inspection revealed a few unsettling clues: a faint trail of blood leading into the nearby woods and a piece of torn fabric caught on a branch, later identified as part of Bob's work uniform.

The police cordoned off the area and initiated a search of the surrounding woods. Search dogs were brought in, but they lost Bob's scent about a mile into the dense forest. The initial search yielded no further evidence, leading to a growing sense of frustration among the investigators.

One of the primary theories considered by the police was that Bob had been abducted. The eyewitness accounts of the mysterious man seen near her car and the blood trail suggested a possible struggle. This theory gained traction when a local resident, Karen Mitchell, came forward with information about a suspicious individual she had seen loitering around the diner in the days leading up to Bob's disappearance. According to Mitchell, the man had an unsettling demeanor and had been asking about the employees' schedules.

Despite this lead, the police were unable to identify the man or find any further evidence linking him to Bob's disappearance. The lack of CCTV footage in the area where her car was found and the absence of additional witnesses made it difficult to advance this theory.

Another theory that emerged was that Bob might have left voluntarily. Friends and family members were quick to dismiss this idea, describing Bob as a responsible and loving individual with no known reasons to abandon her life abruptly. However, the police considered every possibility and looked into her personal life for any signs of distress.

Interviews with her close friends revealed that Bob had been experiencing some financial difficulties and had recently broken up with her boyfriend. Although these factors could suggest a motive for a voluntary disappearance, there was no concrete evidence to support this theory. Bob had made plans to visit her family the following weekend and had not shown any signs of planning to leave permanently.

Given the rising concerns about human trafficking in the region, the police also explored the possibility that Bob had fallen victim to a trafficking ring. The proximity of her disappearance to major highways made this a plausible theory. Similar cases in nearby towns where young women had gone missing under mysterious circumstances added weight to this possibility.

The police collaborated with federal agencies and human trafficking task forces, but no substantial links were found. While this theory could not be entirely ruled out, the lack of concrete evidence again left investigators at a standstill.

The disappearance of Bob Bobo shook the small community to its core. Vigils were held, and search parties were organized by local residents. Flyers bearing Bob's photograph and details were distributed across the county, and her family appeared on local news channels pleading for any information that could lead to her whereabouts.

As days turned into weeks, the hope of finding Bob began to wane, but her family remained steadfast in their search. They hired a private investigator who re-examined the case, conducted independent interviews, and followed up on tips from the public. Despite these efforts, no new significant leads emerged.

The case of Bob Bobo's disappearance remains one of the most perplexing and tragic mysteries the town has ever faced. The lack of definitive evidence and the multitude of possible scenarios have left everyone involved grasping for answers. Each theory, while plausible in its own right, failed to provide a comprehensive explanation for what happened to Bob that fateful night.

In the years that followed, occasional tips and sightings were reported, but none led to any breakthroughs. The case remains open, with Bob's family and the community holding onto a glimmer of hope that one day, the truth will be uncovered, and Bob will be brought home.

————

As the search for answers continues, Bob's memory lives on in the hearts of those who knew and loved her, a beacon of hope amidst the enduring mystery.

# CHAPTER
# FORTY-FIVE
DAMING XU

DAMING XU, a 63-year-old mathematics professor at the University of Oregon, vanished on November 4, 2007, during a solo hike in the Three Sisters Wilderness, Oregon. An experienced hiker and avid outdoor enthusiast, his disappearance left investigators puzzled and his family devastated.

———

On a crisp November morning, Daming Xu set out for a day hike to Olallie Mountain. Known for its challenging trails and breathtaking views, the Three Sisters Wilderness was a favorite destination for Xu and his wife, Shixiu. Equipped with a lightweight jacket, a guidebook, and a water bottle, Xu planned to return home by evening.

Eyewitnesses later reported seeing Xu at the summit of Olallie Mountain around 1:30 PM. A couple who encountered him at the peak mentioned that he appeared hurried, spending only a few minutes before descending. This was the last confirmed sighting of Xu.

When Xu failed to return home, his worried family alerted the authorities. The search operation, led by the Lane County Sheriff's Office, commenced immediately. Xu's white 2003 Chevrolet Impala was found parked at the Olallie trailhead near Bear Flats on November 6. Inside the vehicle were his cell phone, a heavier jacket, and half of the hiking guidebook "100 Hikes in the Central Oregon Cascades" by William Sullivan. The other half, containing the map for Xu's planned route, was discovered in the French Pete Creek drainage area on November 15.

Despite extensive search efforts involving multiple counties, the Oregon National Guard, and the Civil Air Patrol, no additional clues were found in the immediate aftermath of his disappearance. The search teams scoured the dense forest, treacherous terrains, and steep drainages around Olallie Mountain, but Xu remained missing.

Eyewitness accounts played a crucial role in reconstructing Xu's last known movements. The couple who saw him at the summit noted that Xu seemed unusually rushed. This urgency suggested that Xu might have realized he was behind schedule or felt the onset of adverse weather conditions.

Another hiker later found a portion of Xu's guidebook in a steep drainage near French Pete Creek, about seven miles from where Xu was last seen. This discovery narrowed the search area but also highlighted the challenging and dangerous nature of the terrain.

Several theories emerged regarding Xu's disappearance. The most widely accepted hypothesis is that Xu got disoriented and lost his way. Despite being an experienced hiker, the thick forest and rugged landscape of the Three Sisters Wilderness could easily confuse even seasoned outdoorsmen.

- Accidental Injury or Hypothermia: Given Xu's hasty descent and the subsequent change in weather, one theory posits that he may have sustained an injury or succumbed to hypothermia. The dense forest, with its steep drop-offs and fallen trees, poses significant hazards, particularly if one ventures off-trail. The discovery of his guidebook in a creek drainage supports the idea that Xu might have fallen and become incapacitated.

- Wildlife Encounter: Though less likely, the possibility of a dangerous encounter with wildlife cannot be entirely ruled out. The Three Sisters Wilderness is home to bears and other potentially dangerous animals, and an unprepared hiker could find themselves in a perilous situation.

- Foul Play: While there is no concrete evidence to support this theory, some have speculated about the possibility of foul play. The remote location and the fact that no remains or personal items (aside from the guidebook) were found leave room for this speculation. However, the absence of any clear motive or suspects makes this theory less convincing.

Despite the extensive initial search efforts, Xu's case remains unsolved. Over the years, volunteers and professional search teams have periodically resumed the search, hoping to uncover new clues. In 2008, a large-scale search involving 45 volunteers and 400 hours of effort yielded no results. The rugged and inaccessible nature of the terrain around French Pete Creek, where Xu's guidebook was found, continues to be a significant obstacle.

Shixiu, Xu's wife, has expressed her enduring grief and the difficulty of not having any remains to bring closure to the family. The emotional toll on Xu's family and friends has been immense, compounded by the mystery that shrouds his fate.

———

Despite his experience and preparedness, the unforgiving wilderness of the Three Sisters claimed him, leaving behind a trail of questions and heartache. The combination of harsh terrain, adverse weather, and the inherent risks of solo hiking likely contributed to his tragic fate.

# CHAPTER
# FORTY-SIX

RON OHM

THE CASE of Ron Ohm's disappearance has left both authorities and the public grappling for answers. On August 9, 2012, Ron Ohm, a 52-year-old photographer, vanished while hiking in the Mount Jefferson Wilderness, Oregon.

———

Ohm was hiking near Russell Lake with two friends when he decided to venture off alone to take photographs of the scenic landscape. His friends reported that he planned to return within a few hours, but when he failed to come back by the agreed time, they raised the alarm.

Search and rescue teams were deployed immediately, scouring the dense forest and rugged terrain. Helicopters, search dogs, and over 60 volunteers participated in the effort, covering an extensive area around Russell Lake and the surrounding trails. Despite these efforts, no signs of Ohm, his camera, or any of his belongings were discovered.

The police investigation revealed a few critical details and inconsistencies that have fueled various theories. According to Ohm's friends, he was an experienced hiker and familiar with the area, which makes his sudden disappearance all the more puzzling. The terrain around Russell Lake is known for its challenging conditions, but Ohm was well-equipped and prepared for his hike.

Several hikers who were in the area at the time reported seeing Ohm taking photographs along a ridge but didn't notice anything unusual. One hiker mentioned seeing a man matching Ohm's description walking alone in the opposite direction of Russell Lake, towards a less traveled part of the wilderness. This sighting, however, could not be verified, and no additional evidence was found to support this account.

Multiple theories have emerged regarding Ohm's disappearance, each with varying degrees of plausibility.

- Accidental Death: Given the rugged and often treacherous terrain of the Mount Jefferson Wilderness, the most straightforward theory is that Ohm suffered a fatal accident. He could have slipped and fallen into a ravine or creek, his body concealed by the dense underbrush and rocky landscape. However, the lack of any physical evidence—no clothing, camera, or remains—casts doubt on this theory.
- Animal Attack: Another possibility is that Ohm encountered a bear or mountain lion. While such attacks are rare, they are not unheard of in this region. Predatory animals could potentially drag a body away, leaving little trace. Yet, search teams found no signs of a struggle or animal tracks near the area where Ohm was last seen.
- Voluntary Disappearance: Some speculate that Ohm may have chosen to disappear voluntarily, possibly to start a new life

elsewhere. Friends and family, however, refute this idea, citing Ohm's strong ties to his family and his passion for photography and nature, which he would unlikely abandon without notice.

- Foul Play: There is also the theory of foul play. Ohm could have encountered someone with ill intentions. This theory gained some traction when an unconfirmed report surfaced about a transient seen near the trailhead around the time of Ohm's disappearance. However, no concrete evidence or suspects have emerged from this line of investigation.

- Supernatural or Paranormal Explanations: Some have ventured into more fantastical explanations, suggesting supernatural or paranormal involvement. The Mount Jefferson Wilderness has a reputation for mysterious disappearances and strange occurrences, leading to speculation about otherworldly forces at play. These theories, while intriguing, lack any scientific basis and remain in the realm of folklore.

Despite the official search being called off after several weeks, Ohm's family and friends have continued their efforts to find him. They have organized multiple search parties and used social media to keep the public engaged and informed about any new developments. The case has also garnered attention from true crime enthusiasts and paranormal investigators, further keeping the mystery alive in public discourse.

Documentaries and articles have explored Ohm's disappearance, adding layers of speculation and analysis. One notable documentary drew parallels between Ohm's case and other unexplained disappearances in national parks across the United States, suggesting a pattern that authorities might be overlooking.

———

With no solid evidence to point to his fate, theories and speculations will continue to thrive. As the years go by, the hope of finding Ohm diminishes.

# FORTY-SEVEN
## ERIC LEWIS

ON THE MORNING of July 1, 2010, experienced climber Eric Lewis, 57, went missing under mysterious circumstances while ascending the Gibraltar Ledges route on Mount Rainier. Eric was part of a three-man climbing team, including Don Storm Jr. and Trevor Lane, both of whom were less experienced compared to Eric.

The team encountered severe weather conditions with high winds and low visibility, which played a crucial role in the ensuing events.

At approximately 13,900 feet, Don and Trevor paused to wait for Eric, who was the last climber on the rope line. When they pulled the rope in, they discovered only a coil with a butterfly knot and no sign of Eric. They had seen glimpses of him moments before but now found only a void where he should have been. The immediate area was searched thoroughly by Don and Trevor, but their limited experience and the harsh weather conditions hampered their efforts. Believing Eric might have somehow bypassed them, they proceeded to the summit ridge but found no trace of him. Eventually, they descended to Camp Muir, the high camp at 10,200 feet, and reported Eric's disappearance to the park rangers.

The search for Eric Lewis was extensive and involved multiple agencies and resources. On July 1st, climbing ranger Tom Payne and two mountain guides quickly ascended from Camp Muir to the summit area, searching for any sign of Eric but finding nothing. By the afternoon of July 2nd, over 40 personnel were involved in the search, including National Park Service climbing rangers, climbing guides from Rainier Mountaineering, Alpine Ascents International, and International Mountain Guides, as well as volunteers from Olympic Mountain Rescue.

A military CH-47 Chinook helicopter from Fort Lewis

and a commercial helicopter from Northwest Helicopters assisted with aerial searches. Ground searchers located Eric's backpack, climbing harness, and snow shovel at 13,600 feet, and a small snow cave at 13,800 feet. Despite the extensive search efforts, which included scouring the upper Nisqually and Ingraham Glaciers and the summit rim steam caves, no further clues were found. Incident Commander Glenn Kessler noted the high-elevation glacial terrain required significant technical skill and posed risks to the searchers, leading to a scale-back in efforts as the likelihood of finding Eric alive diminished.

The disappearance of Eric Lewis has spawned numerous theories, some of which are grounded in the harsh realities of mountain climbing, while others verge on the speculative.

- Hypothermia and Disorientation: One plausible theory is that Eric, suffering from hypothermia, became confused and disoriented. Hypothermia can cause impaired judgment and odd behavior, which might explain why he unclipped from the rope. The discovery of his backpack and snow cave suggests he attempted to create a temporary shelter but was ultimately unable to survive the conditions.
- Voluntary Separation: Another theory is that Eric, facing a personal issue or feeling a

burden to his less experienced companions, chose to unclip intentionally. This is less likely but not entirely dismissible given the stressful environment and potential psychological factors at play.

- Foul Play: Although there is no concrete evidence to support foul play, some have speculated that Eric's companions might have had a role in his disappearance. The circumstances of his unclipping and the subsequent events have led to questions about the thoroughness of the initial search by his partners. However, without evidence, this remains speculative.

- Equipment Failure: The possibility of equipment failure, such as a faulty carabiner or rope issue, cannot be entirely ruled out. However, given Eric's experience and the lack of physical evidence suggesting equipment failure, this theory is less favored.

The official investigation by the National Park Service and other authorities focused on gathering all available evidence and eyewitness testimonies. The search involved methodical tracking of possible paths Eric could have taken and examining the area for any signs of his whereabouts. The harsh weather conditions and the challenging terrain significantly limited the investigation's scope and effectiveness.

Authorities interviewed Don Storm Jr. and Trevor Lane extensively, both of whom maintained that Eric had unclipped himself and they had conducted a thorough search immediately after realizing he was missing. Their accounts were consistent, and no discrepancies were found that could suggest foul play. The investigation also reviewed Eric's equipment and climbing history, affirming that he was well-versed in climbing but had chosen to pack light for this expedition, which may have contributed to his vulnerability in severe weather conditions.

Eric Lewis's disappearance has been the subject of various articles and discussions in mountaineering and mystery forums. Some draw parallels to other famous mountaineering incidents where climbers have gone missing or made life-and-death decisions under extreme conditions. The case remains a topic of speculation and debate, with some suggesting supernatural or psychological explanations.

Theories will continue to circulate, but without new evidence, Eric Lewis's fate remains a haunting enigma in the annals of mountaineering history.

# CHAPTER
# FORTY-EIGHT
## KARIN ELIZABETH MERO

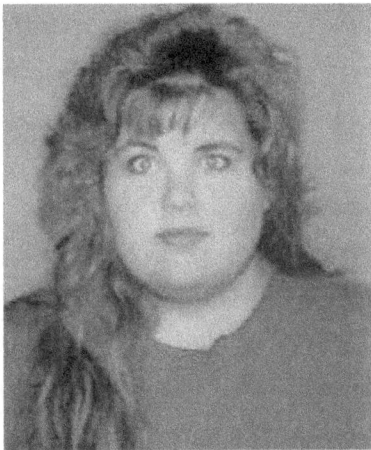

KARIN ELIZABETH MERO, born on May 21, 1969, disappeared under mysterious circumstances from McCloud, California, on February 15, 1997.

Karin Mero, who had undergone a liver transplant in 1994, required regular anti-rejection medication to survive. At the time of her disappearance, she was 27 years old, stood 5'8" tall, and weighed 170 pounds. She had brown hair, green eyes, and distinctive scars: one on her face near her nose and another on her lower abdomen from her surgery.

Karin was last seen on the front porch of Ed Henline Sr.'s residence on East Minnesota Avenue in McCloud, where she had been living with her boyfriend, Ed Henline Jr. She vanished without a trace, leaving behind no signs of struggle or departure plans. Initially, Karin's absence went unreported for eight months. Her parents and authorities believed she had left voluntarily due to an outstanding warrant for her arrest and her estrangement from her husband.

The Siskiyou County Sheriff's Office eventually listed Karin as a missing person in October 1997. By this time, the delay in reporting had significantly hindered the investigation. Detectives, led by Det. Jesus Fernandez, were tasked with unraveling the mystery. Karin's medical condition and her dependence on anti-rejection medication added urgency to the case.

The police learned that Karin's only income came from a $700 monthly disability payment. With her medications left behind and no access to her funds, the theory of voluntary disappearance became increasingly unlikely.

Multiple accounts placed Karin on the front porch of the Henline residence on the day she disappeared. However, no one reported seeing her leave or noticing anything unusual. The Henlines, particularly Ed Sr. and Ed Jr., were scrutinized closely. The Henlines were known in the community and had been involved in legal troubles before. Their connection to Karin and their questionable activities raised suspicions.

Ed Henline Sr. and Ed Henline Jr. were not just casual acquaintances; they were deeply entwined in Karin's life. After Karin's disappearance, both Henlines were accused of writing fraudulent checks on her bank account. Furthermore, in 1999, they faced drug charges, adding to their dubious reputation.

In a strange twist, another young woman, Hannah Zaccaglini, disappeared from the same area four months after Karin. Both women had last been seen at the Henline residence. In 2012, the Henlines were charged with Hannah's murder, although the charges were dropped in 2013 due to lack of evidence. The parallels between the two cases fueled speculation that the Henlines were involved in both disappearances.

Initially, some believed Karin had left voluntarily to escape her troubled life. This theory was supported by her existing warrant and her strained personal relationships. However, this theory lost credibility as time passed without any sightings or contact from Karin.

The most prevailing theory involves foul play, potentially at the hands of the Henlines. Given their history of criminal behavior, including financial fraud and drug offenses, and their direct connection to both missing women, many suspect they were involved in Karin's disappearance. The fraudulent checks written on Karin's account after her disappearance add weight to this theory.

Another theory suggests that Karin might have been involved in a drug-related incident. The Henlines' arrest on drug charges shortly after her disappearance supports this possibility. If Karin was involved in or witnessed illegal activities, it could have led to her being silenced.

Despite the passage of time, Karin Mero's case remains open. The Siskiyou County Sheriff's Office continues to receive tips and follow leads. Public interest in the case persists, partly due to the eerie similarities with Hannah Zaccaglini's disappearance. Media coverage and online forums have kept the cases in the public eye, prompting occasional new information.

———

The disappearance of Karin Elizabeth Mero is a tragic and perplexing case. The delay in reporting her missing, the suspicious activities of those close to her, and the subsequent disappearance of another young woman from the same locale all contribute to a complex web of theories and unanswered questions. As of now, Karin remains missing, and her case stands as a somber reminder of the challenges faced in missing person investigations.

# FORTY-NINE
ROY STEPHENS

THE DISAPPEARANCE of Roy Stephens is a haunting mystery that has perplexed investigators and family members since that fateful night on November 16, 2005. Roy, a devoted husband and father, vanished under circumstances that remain unclear despite extensive investigations.

———

Roy Stephens, a 48-year-old Caucasian male with gray hair and green eyes, was last seen at a local bar in Crescent, Oregon. He had spent several hours with friends after work and called his wife at 11:00 p.m. to inform her that he was on his way home. Roy was wearing a black leather jacket, a white t-shirt, blue jeans, and insulated boots. However, he never arrived home and was never heard from again.

Nine days later, on Thanksgiving Day, November 24, 2005, hikers discovered Roy's gray 1991 Ford Taurus on Waldo Lake Road, approximately 10-15 miles from his home. The car was found in an area completely opposite of his intended route. Inside the vehicle, Roy's wallet and paycheck were found on the passenger seat, and there was vomit next to the car, raising immediate concerns.

The initial investigation involved three different law enforcement agencies: Lane County, Klamath County, and the Willamette National Forest authorities. This jurisdictional complexity hindered the search efforts. Only four hours of searching were conducted initially, and no cadaver dogs were deployed, even months after Roy's disappearance.

Roy's family, particularly his wife Marilyn, who had recently undergone triple-bypass surgery, and their son, searched the area near the Odell Lake Lodge but found no trace of him. Marilyn reached out to neighbors and friends, but no one had seen Roy since the night he disappeared.

Eyewitness accounts suggest that Roy left the tavern and intended to stop by a friend's house before heading home. However, his car being found in a different direction led to several theories. One theory posits that Roy was disoriented, possibly due to alcohol or drug use, leading him to drive in the wrong direction. His daughter, Krista Dolby, mentioned that Roy had a history of drug abuse and associated with unsavory individuals, which might have played a role in his disappearance.

Another theory suggests foul play. The presence of Roy's wallet and paycheck in the car implies that robbery was not a motive. Some speculate that Roy may have been attacked and left in the wilderness, but the absence of any physical evidence or forensic testing of the car leaves this theory unconfirmed.

The community's response to Roy's disappearance was notably lacking. Despite efforts by the family to organize a search, local law enforcement deemed it unsafe for them to venture up the mountain. No volunteers from the community stepped forward to assist in the search, leading to speculation about Roy's standing within the community and whether he had made any enemies.

Several possible scenarios have been proposed regarding Roy's fate:

- Accidental Disorientation: Roy might have become disoriented, stopped the car, vomited, and wandered into the wilderness, where he succumbed to the elements or a wildlife attack.
- Foul Play: Given the strange circumstances of his car's location and the lack of personal items taken, foul play remains a strong possibility. Theories include conflicts with the last people he was supposed to visit or an unknown assailant.
- Voluntary Disappearance: Although unlikely, given his close ties to his family, some suggest Roy might have chosen to disappear, leaving behind his personal items to mislead investigators.

Fifteen years after his disappearance, no trace of Roy Stephens has been found. The case remains open but cold, with law enforcement agencies still lacking any solid leads or evidence. The mysterious nature of his disappearance continues to haunt his family and the community, leaving many questions unanswered.

---

The disappearance of Roy Stephens is a tragic and puzzling case that highlights the complexities and challenges of missing person investigations, especially in

areas with overlapping jurisdictions and sparse popula-
tions. Despite the various theories and sporadic search
efforts, Roy's fate remains unknown, a silent echo in the
dense forests of Oregon. His family continues to seek
closure, holding onto the hope that one day, the truth
will emerge from the shadows.

# CHAPTER
# FIFTY

GRACE ELAN SABOTS

GRACE ELAN SABOTS, a 27-year-old woman from Portland, Oregon, disappeared under mysterious circumstances on March 1, 2014, while camping in Siskiyou County, California. Her case remains unsolved, shrouded in ambiguity and raising numerous questions.

———

Grace Elan Sabots was originally from Oakland, California, but had lived in Portland, Oregon, for several years before her disappearance. She co-owned a house-cleaning business and was known for her adventurous spirit and love for the outdoors. On March 1, 2014, she embarked on a solo camping trip near the Klamath River in Siskiyou County, a location known for its scenic beauty and remote, rugged terrain.

Grace was last seen by a Siskiyou County sheriff's deputy on March 1, 2014. The deputy encountered her at a campsite along State Route 96 near the Klamath River. At the time, she appeared to be in good health and did not seem to require any assistance. The deputy noted that she was alone at the campsite and left shortly after ensuring she was safe.

The following morning, at approximately 8:30 AM, the same deputy discovered Grace's light blue 1989 Toyota Corolla abandoned near the Skeahan River Bar Access area, about eight miles east of Interstate 5. The vehicle's location, coupled with the discovery of fresh footprints leading into the river but not returning, prompted immediate concern for her safety.

An extensive search was launched, involving the Siskiyou County Sheriff's Office Search and Rescue Team, a California Highway Patrol helicopter, and various volunteers. The search spanned several miles along the Klamath River and surrounding areas but yielded no substantial clues. Divers scoured the river, and canine units were deployed, yet no trace of Grace was found beyond the initial footprints.

Eyewitness accounts are sparse in this case. Apart from the deputy's sighting, no other confirmed interactions with Grace were reported in the days leading up to her disappearance. However, passersby later reported seeing sheriff's deputies working inside crime scene tape around the area of Skeahan Bar, indicating a high level of concern and the seriousness with which the authorities treated the case.

Several theories have been proposed regarding Grace's disappearance:

- Accidental Drowning: The most straightforward theory is that Grace, possibly trying to get closer to the river for water or exploration, slipped and fell into the river, resulting in accidental drowning. The lack of returning footprints supports this theory, although no body was ever recovered despite thorough searches.
- Foul Play: Another theory suggests that Grace may have encountered foul play. Given the isolated nature of the area, it's conceivable that

she could have been attacked or abducted by someone familiar with the remote terrain. However, there is no direct evidence to support this theory, and no suspects have been identified.

- Voluntary Disappearance: Some speculate that Grace may have chosen to disappear voluntarily. This theory is less likely given her established life and business in Portland, and the lack of any known personal issues that might drive such a decision.
- Wildlife Encounter: The region is home to various wildlife, including bears and mountain lions. An encounter with a wild animal could have resulted in her injury or death, but again, no physical evidence such as clothing or remains were found to support this.

Grace's disappearance remains an active investigation. The Siskiyou County Sheriff's Department continues to encourage anyone with information to come forward. Over the years, the case has garnered attention from various true crime communities and forums, such as Websleuths and the Charley Project, where amateur sleuths discuss potential leads and theories.

———

The case of Grace Elan Sabots is a haunting reminder of the dangers that can accompany outdoor adventures in remote areas and one of Siskiyou County's enduring mysteries.

# AFTERWORD

As we close *Lost Souls: 50 National Park Disappearances*, we are left with a profound sense of mystery and contemplation. The stories of these missing individuals are a stark reminder of the unpredictable and often unforgiving nature of the wilderness. They also highlight the limitations and challenges faced by search and rescue teams, despite their dedication and expertise.

Throughout this book, we have explored a range of cases, each with its unique circumstances and unanswered questions. From the dense forests of Yosemite to the vast expanse of the Grand Canyon, these national parks are places of awe-inspiring beauty but also of great peril. The disappearances chronicled here serve as a sobering testament to the risks inherent in venturing into the wild.

One of the most poignant aspects of these cases is the

enduring hope and determination of the families and friends left behind. Their tireless efforts to seek answers, often against overwhelming odds, are a testament to the human spirit. In many instances, the search for loved ones continues long after official efforts have ceased, driven by a profound need for closure and understanding.

The issue of missing persons in national parks has also sparked important discussions about policy and accountability. Advocates like Heidi Streetman have campaigned for better tracking and reporting mechanisms to ensure that these cases are not forgotten and that lessons can be learned to prevent future tragedies. The introduction of legislative measures, such as the TRACE Act, represents a step in the right direction, aiming to enhance the sharing of information and improve search efforts on federal lands.

As we reflect on these stories, it is essential to recognize the balance between preserving the natural beauty of our national parks and ensuring the safety of those who explore them. Education and preparedness are key components in preventing such disappearances. Visitors should be equipped with the knowledge and tools necessary to navigate these environments safely, while park authorities must continue to refine and improve their search and rescue capabilities.

In closing, *Lost Souls: 50 National Park Disappearances* is not just a collection of mysteries; it is a call to action. It urges us to remember those who have vanished and to support efforts to enhance safety and accountability in our national parks. It is a reminder of the delicate interplay between human ambition and nature's vast, untamed wilderness.

May the stories within these pages inspire us to tread carefully, respect the power of the natural world, and never lose sight of the importance of finding and protecting those who are lost.

- Even Grant

If you enjoyed this book, continue with other great books from
FREE REIGN PUBLISHING

# ABOUT THE AUTHOR

Evan Grant is a multi-faceted individual known for his work in the fields of writing, conservation, and public advocacy. With a deep passion for the natural world, Grant has dedicated much of his career to highlighting the importance of preserving wilderness areas and protecting wildlife. His writing often explores themes related to the environment, blending factual reporting with compelling storytelling to raise awareness about critical conservation issues.

Grant's work has earned him recognition for its impact on public policy and environmental protection efforts. He has contributed to various publications, where his insightful articles and essays have informed and inspired a wide audience. Grant is actively involved in numerous environmental organizations, advocating for sustainable practices and the protection of endangered species.

With a background that combines environmental science and activism, Grant continues to be a prominent voice in the fight for a healthier planet. His commitment to these causes is reflected in his ongoing efforts to educate and engage the public, ensuring that the beauty and biodiversity of our natural world are preserved for future generations.

## ALSO BY FREE REIGN PUBLISHING

WENDIGO CHRONICLES

MYSTERIES IN THE FOREST

STORIES FROM THE NICU

CRAZY MEDICAL STORIES

PAWSITIVE MOMENTS: LIFE IN A VETERINARY CLINIC

STORIES FROM THE NICU

VANISHED: STRANGE & MYSTERIOUS DISAPPEARANCES

DIAGNOSIS: RARE MEDICAL CASES